Always shine your light!

-Laura Dillard

MW00598122

WARD OF THE STATE

A MEMOIR OF FOSTER CARE

Karlos Dillard

Ward of the State Subtitle

© 2020 by Karlos Dillard

All rights reserved. This book or any portion thereof may not be reproduced or used in any manner whatsoever without the express written permission of the publisher except for the use of brief quotations in a book review.

ISBN (Print): 978-1-54399-902-0
ISBN (eBook): 978-1-54399-903-7

This book is dedicated to my life coach, mentor and proclaimed father Perry Morgan. You showed me tough love and taught me how to accept my blessings and favor from God. I love you for showing me how to love myself.

Also dedicated to Pauline Rickey "It is during our darkest moments that we must focus to see the light" Aristotle

About the Author

Most known for his appearances on Cut.com a viral Youtube Production company based out of Seattle, Karlos has made a name for himself making people laugh while addressing social issues. Using his large social media platforms, Karlos has brought attention to Black gun ownership and police brutality. He is a Commerical Actor and Model working with the nation's top photographers like National Geographic Photographer Art Wolfe. He has also appeared in commercials for companies such as Microsoft, Amazon and Mercedes Benz. Karlos has also advocated for other foster children currently in the system, doing public speaking engagements like Seattle Ignite 40 with his talk "Friend of a Foster Child". Karlos resides in Seattle Wa with his husband and their two dogs. He has dedicated his life to shading light onto dark spaces in society and to be a voice for those that haven't found theirs.

Contents

1

Where is Mom?

It was the last day of school in the second grade. A day when children dream about the wonders they will encounter during the summer. Family trips, carnivals and amusement parks, and all the things summer is filled with. The smell of the summer breeze is gracing its way through the dunes, pushing glass-like sand against your legs as you run on the beach. There will be a gathering of loved ones at the annual family reunion, where you can be sure your uncle will start a debate trying to prove he's the smartest. These dreams and those kids, none of them exist in my summer.

Looking out the window of Roosevelt Elementary, I see the same thing I had seen all year, the ghetto. The trash scattered streets, under-booked and overworked hookers on the corner. This neighborhood once had prestigious lawns and beautiful two-story homes. The upper-middle class had once walked these same streets, smiling as they wave to their neighbors while sending their children off to school.

Those lawns are now lots. Dirty needle filled lots. Last year, a faggot was raped, beaten, and then thugs forced a broom up his rectum. The police found his body only two lots over from my house. The neighborhood that was once the home for white people who smiled as they walked down the street was now run by gangs. And the bright smiles have become smiles rotted by the use of drugs and booze. The homes are now Section 8 sub-developments. Four bedrooms and two baths homes were converted into two bedroom and one bath apartments. Only a thin, cheap layer of drywall separated the apartments. You'd hear everything your neighbors did. The fights. The woman screaming for her children as her boyfriend beat them all. Her moaning from pain as she nursed her family back to health. And the nasty make-up sex she had with him, as he kissed her wounds oh so gently. One might think that I just had a very well-developed imagination, and I made up stories from the noises I heard. I knew because those were my walls. That woman was my mother and that man, he was Satan's spawn, always beating everyone, then enjoying the entire family sexually.

As an eight-year-old, my school is my sanctuary - my escape from the dangers that are outside of the barbed wire fence. One of the only places where you will still see a white face. I prayed every night, hoping my prayers would be answered and I would wake up white in a white family, all happy and content. My teacher, Miss Chimney, was the most beautiful, white woman I had ever seen. In my dreams, she plays the role of my mother. She bakes bonbons for the holidays and we sing carols in front of the tree. She's my superhero of sorts, always there for my brother and I.

RING!

That's the bell, the final one for the year. Everyone rushes to unpack their desks, the ones that lift up giving you a false sense of privacy. All year long I stole my classmates' snacks, stuffing them in my backpack to save for dinner. I was the first out of the classroom. I hardly had any school supplies so packing up was pretty easy for me.

My older brother, Tim, met me outside the school by the flag. Timothy is the second youngest. And he and I are the closest out of the four of us. Because we have different fathers, you would never guess that we were brothers. Tim was in the third grade and the complete opposite of me. He is a pretty big kid and already wore a men's size nine in shoes. Although he is big for his age, he is not a fighter. He is more of a nerd who likes playing with *Pokemon* cards and playing hide and seek. All of the neighborhood kids teased him because of his light skin.

As we walked home, I didn't have that exciting feeling of summer. Instead, hunger and the fear of the unknown filled me. Since tomorrow was Tim's birthday, maybe mama would be there with a party! My mother had not been home for some time, and we were running out of food. Shit, just last week we had to fight a gas station attendant to save Tim from getting arrested for stealing pop tarts. Our house was only three blocks from the school, which I loved. Being so close to our school made it easier to walk there in the cold Michigan winters. I cannot stand winter. Of course, I loved Christmas and the first snowfall but I never had adequate clothing for any of those activities. Yet, in the summer heat, it was also very convenient to be close to school. When we arrived home, the door was locked. This was not unusual because our older sister, Jatia, who was thirteen years old, was the only one who had a key. Tim and I waited for about an hour then decided to head back to the school. This one small decision would change my life and the lives of all my family members.

Once we were back at the school we went to see if Miss Chimney was still there. We caught her just as she was closing her door for the summer. Miss Chimney seemed surprised to see us and greeted us with a smile like always. Tim and I told her about being locked out of the house and waiting. After learning why we were at the school her smile became a frown and she instructed us to sit in her classroom while she made a phone call. Those minutes she was gone seemed like an eternity. Tim suggested that Miss Chimney could take us to her house until our mom came back. Miss Chimney was no stranger to our mother. She often dropped by on Saturdays to take Tim out on adventures. My mind started making glorious scenarios of how Miss Chimney would let Tim and I live with her, and we would go to the zoo and on all these amazing field trips.

Those illusions were quickly eradicated when I saw two police officers and a young white woman in a grey tweed dress enter the room. Miss Chimney was the last one to enter the room with the same worried expression on her face. Miss Chimney told us that the woman and the policeman were here to help us. From growing up in the ghetto of Muskegon Heights, even at a young age I knew what they were there for. Plus, it happened to my cousin a few months ago. A few weeks before, our cousin was removed by the government and put into foster care. It had been happening a lot in the neighborhood, especially to the kids whose parents were on drugs or selling them. The lady in the grey dress introduced herself as Miss Jennifer. She is a white lady in her late twenties with shoulder-length, auburn hair. She told Tim and I she would be our case worker. She then asked us to repeat the story we had given to Miss Chimney. Tim refused to talk to her. Then, she turned to me, kneeling to my level and asked me to tell her. I told her my sister should be home and we would just go back home. This Jennifer lady suggested I take her home with me so she could get a chance to meet Jatia.

Once outside the school, the policemen who accompanied Miss Jennifer shoved Tim and I into the back of an unmarked Ford Taurus. It wasn't a police car exactly, but I definitely felt suffocated and cramped even with my small bony stature. I started to panic and was very afraid of what would happen next. Although living in the hood, I was pretty tough but at this moment my true innocence was shown as I burst into tears asking for my momma. Tim said nothing. He showed no emotion as he sat in his seat cold and withdrawn.

The car stopped a few houses down from ours and Jennifer instructed us to ask Jatia to come out. That request did not seem too bad and I knew my sister would fix this. My fear subsided as we inched closer to our house. Even Tim seemed to have a pep in his step traveling to the door. We were steps away when I glanced behind my shoulder to see two black vans pulling up next to Miss Jennifer's car. Time seemed to stop almost, but so many things happened in that pause in time. It happened in a flash. Jatia opened the door with the chain still attached and the black vans screeched to a halt in front of our house, Men in all black piled out with guns drawn and burst through the door. My world was spinning with shouts and demands from these people. I truly felt as if we were in a war zone. They gathered all three of my siblings and I into a corner while they searched the house. My mind was working so fast and life became a fog. I shut down, closing my eyes and letting the noise subside. This was my safe place, a place in my mind where I can remove myself from my physical surroundings. My safe place was nowhere but everywhere and easily accessible.

2

Devil's Spawn

My earliest memory is my second birthday. I remember that day like it was yesterday. I got a tricycle and momma threw a party. Life was different when I was that age. My father worked and my mother stayed at home. This memory stands out because it was the first time I saw my father do drugs.

At this time, my dad was in his early twenties. He was six feet tall and slender. He has almond shaped eyes and glowing brown skin. His name was Carlos Sr. I was his only child and named after him. A lot of people call me his twin because we look so much alike. Similar to my father, I have a larger than life personality and a smile to match it. I didn't know then but my dad was a gang member and a drug dealer. He met my mom through my Uncle Feeky who was in the same gang. He and my uncle were smoking green smelly stuff and sniffing powdery stuff that looked like flour. That was the last memory I have of my father for years of my life. Soon after my party, my parents broke up. After my mom and dad broke up I didn't see much of my dad for a couple of years. We moved from house to house and my mom always had different men in and out of the house.

My mother soon began dating a man named Deon when I was five years old. He drove a nice car and always smelled good. This man seemed to be perfect, but little did I know he would single-handedly destroy my family. The first incident happened one night I was sleeping in my mom's room. I was awakened by my mother's scream as she pleaded for him to stop. I hopped out of bed and exited the dark room. When I entered the living room, I saw Deon on top of my mom punching her in the face. He was muttering something about her stealing his coke between the blows. I had seen my mother fight my father, but never like this. Something inside of me exploded, I felt like a bomb went off. All of the anger I had been compressing made it's way to the surface, I jumped on Deon's back and bit him. Screaming in pain he threw me against the wall expelling the air I had in my lungs. My mom seemed to find strength and pushed him off of her, only to be slapped to the ground again. I crawled to my sister's room and woke her up with terror in my eyes. Jumping right to her feet, she told me to hide under her bed as she left the room. I crawled all the way to the back of the bed and tried to listen the best I could. Seconds later I heard grunting and ping sounds. It sounded like a frying pan hitting hard. Not knowing what to do, I climbed out of my hiding place and went back into the living room. I saw Jatia with a skillet in her hand beating Deon. My mom got up and started yelling for Jatia to stop, and ran over and pushed her down. Jatia came back into her room sweaty and breathing hard. She locked her door and told me I could sleep with her for the night.

After that night, every time my mom did something to get Deon mad, he beat her. I guess my mom wasn't a good enough punching bag because he started hitting my siblings and I. One night after I heard him beat mom, he came into my room and told me to go into the basement. I did as I was told while mentally getting ready to take the blows to my body that most certainly would be coming. But instead he was sitting on the couch watching TV. I made my way to the couch with my head down looking at the floor. I sat next to him and looked at the TV. He was watching porn. I knew what this was because my brothers would sneak into my mom's room and watch it with their friends. I sat there watching the screen. The woman was putting a man's penis in her mouth and moving her head up and down. I felt pressure on the back of my head. And when I looked at Deon, he had his pants down to his ankles. He forced my head down to his penis and told me to open my mouth. I shook my head no as my stomach turned from the ripe musky smell that came from his private area. In the next instance the left side of my face was warm from the blood running to it from the slap I had received. Deon told me to do what the girl was doing on TV or he would beat the shit out of me and my mother. His penis tasted salty because of the tears running down my cheeks as he shoved it deeper and deeper down my throat. This was the first time I discovered my safe place. Nothing or no one could hurt me here. I took my mental self away from the situation while my physical body was there for his enjoyment.

Our midnight meetings began to happen more often and progressed to Deon finding other entrances into my body. I hated what he did to me, the embarrassment and the pain. After a few months, the physical pain in my rectum went away as well as my innocence. I became cold and withdrawn. I started acting out and getting into fights with the neighborhood kids. I dared not tell my mother because I knew that either she would get beat or she would end up beating me. I cried every night wishing for a new life, hoping one day I could be safe and happy with a perfect family.

The police must have found what they were looking for because I was jolted back to reality by the sound of my sister screaming. She was asking why they had kicked our door open? Why they had guns in our faces? She shielded us behind her as they searched our kitchen. It had been days since my mother had been home and weeks since she had been grocery shopping. All we had left were canned beans and beef-flavored Ramen noodles in the pantry. The fridge was not any better with old crusty, peanut butter and moldy bread. My sister did her best to keep us as well-fed as she could. Every morning we woke up before the sun to travel around our neighborhood looking for soda cans. The four of us looked everywhere, spreading out to knock on doors asking if the residents wanted to donate their cans. We often were able to return the cans at Walmart and score about ten dollars. I was content because that was my normal. I knew some kids had better lives, parents, and houses with white picket fences. But this was my normal. I knew no other lifestyle.

The men in black piled my siblings and I into Miss Jennifer's car and we left. Jatia sat in the middle of the back seat still screaming and asking why. I turned and looked behind me and I saw my house fading away. A part of me was very relieved and the other was worried for what the future held. Could my dreams really be happening? Was my nightmare over? I bubbled with excitement as these questions whirled through my mind. After my brain settled down, I suddenly remembered my mother. Where is she? Did she know we were moving? Naïve and hopeful, I looked out of the window at my new world.

3

First Night in Foster Care

Miss Jennifer drove us to downtown Muskegon, where all the white people lived. And we made our way through the maze of subdivisions. I recognized this part of town because my uncle Tyrone worked at a factory near here. As I was gathering my bearings, the car came to a stop at a beautiful, three-story home with an older black woman standing out front. Miss Jennifer got out of the car and instructed us to do the same. I was the first to respond to her request and I made my way to the stoop to see the woman. My siblings did not cooperate so easily. Jatia and Alex, the two oldest, protested and would not enter the house. In that same instance, I saw my uncle Tyrone walking down the street headed toward us. I screamed for him and we made eye contact. He instantaneously began to sprint to our location. Once Tyrone reached the house he began to ask Jatia and Alex what had happened and why were we there. Jatia seemed to gain courage and began to explain to Tyrone what had happened. In the middle of her explanation, she was interrupted by the officers who had accompanied Ms. Jennifer. The officers shoved us all into the house.

From the porch, I could hear them tell my uncle that we were removed from the custody of our mother and were now temporary wards of the state. That is all I heard of their conversation because my attention was averted by a voice I did not recognize. I traveled into the house and found my way into the kitchen where I found my siblings, Miss Jennifer and the foster woman all sitting around the table. The woman was very kind looking with a twinkle in her eye. She had nice caramel skin and curly black hair. Amidst my state of admiration, the lady introduced herself as Miss Caroline and welcomed us to milk and cookies. I gladly accepted her offer. Jatia, on the other hand, smacked my hand and told me not to take anything from anyone. Ms. Jennifer's face was in pure shock and she asked Jatia to meet her outside. Jatia looked at me and gave me her usual look of "I mean business" and left the room.

Jatia was my favorite sibling, and she always looked out for me. Ever since I could remember, she was there for me for everything. Mom was either gone physically, emotionally or mentally - but not Jatia. I could always rely on my big sister to take care of me. So, when she gives me that look, I listen because of respect.

This whole time I kind of forgot that my brothers were also here. I looked to my right to see Alex rubbing one of his school erasers up and down his arm. He always did this when he's in trouble or scared. Last year when Mama cracked his head open with a buckle, Alex ended up with really bad burns on his arms from being nervous all the time. I grabbed the eraser and threw it. I hated seeing him do that to himself. Miss Caroline got up from her seat and grabbed the eraser off the floor. When she walked up to me, I flinched, expecting a blow. But unexpectedly, she asked us if we wanted to see our rooms. None of us responded even though I was a little excited. Miss Caroline shuffled us down a hallway full of pictures on the wall. Most pictures were of a boy and girl. As we made our way down the hall I noticed the kids grew in the pictures the further we went. I asked her if those were her kids. Miss Caroline smiled and said that they were former wards of the state, but she adopted them. Before I could ask any more questions, she opened the door to our right. The room was bright blue with football stuff everywhere. She had football pillows and stickers on the wall as well as a bed shaped like a football. As I walked into the room, I looked at the bed and frowned. Miss Caroline asked me what was wrong. I shook my head and looked at the floor. She came over and kneeled down beside me and whispered in my ear that it was ok. I looked into her eyes to see if this was a trick. My mom would always do this to me. Asked me if I was ok and if I said no, she would slap me. Could I trust Miss Caroline? Of course not! The only person in this world that I could trust was Jatia. She has always had my best interest at heart.

At the same moment Jatia entered the room, seeming to be in a better mood than when she left. She took my hand and walked me to the bed. Miss Caroline must have noticed that Jatia wanted privacy with me because she let herself out and closed the door behind her. Jatia sat me down on the bed. When I looked into her eyes, they were red and puffy with water still pooling at the crease. My stomach dropped with shock and amazement because I had never seen my sister shed actual tears. Even when my mom dragged her through the house by her hair while whipping here with a cable wire, she didn't cry. Jatia would never shed a tear. She would just take it with sadness in her eyes. She is the strongest out of the four of us, and always made sure we were protected. What had happened to make her cry?

After our moment on the bed, Jatia left the room for a moment and returned with a blanket and pillow. She never spoke of her sadness or the tears she shed. She made a pallet and laid down next to the bed. I crawled into the football bed and closed my eyes. My mind began to wander as I took in the day's events. So much had happened. This morning, we left the house early to snatch some pop tarts from the corner store. Now, I'm in this strange house sleeping in a football bed. Where is my mom? Where are my aunts and uncles? I fell asleep with a mind full of question and no answers.

I was jolted out of sleep by the sound of shouting. I sat up in bed bewildered, forgetting I was in a different house than mine. Catching my bearings, I crawled out and noticed Jatia's pallet was empty. Panicking, I rushed up the stairs afraid she had left me like mom did. As I made my way to the lit living room, it took a couple of seconds for my eyes to adjust from the darkness to the light. When I gained my vision back, I saw my momma standing in the doorway with my uncle Tyrone. They were trying to force their way past Miss Caroline. Everyone was now in the living room and we were shouting for our mother.

After a couple of moments, Miss Caroline let my mother in while informing her that she would call the police if she tried to take us. I looked at my mom and she did not look like I remembered. It had been at least a couple of weeks since I had seen her. She had left the house two weeks before we were taken. Her eyes were dull and withdrawn. And her once beautiful smile was visibly fading. She wrapped me in a hug and told me that she was going to get us back from the system. At this point I did not know what to think because the last time she touched me she was beating the life out of me. Now she wants to fight for me? Not knowing what to do, I unwrapped myself and ran. Jatia told me to go back downstairs. I did as I was told but I tried my hardest to hear what was being said. With no success, I went back to my room and waited for Jatia to come back. When she returned she looked even worse than when we first fell asleep. Once again, nothing was said about what had happened upstairs. As I was falling back to sleep, I asked her when we were going home. Her response was probably never.

Today's date was June 14, 2001. I remember that date and it is engraved in me. It's like an anniversary except without the joy and presents.

The next morning when we awoke, Miss Caroline asked us to bathe. Then, after our baths we could go in the backyard and jump on the trampoline. We did just that. And for the first time since I can remember I actually felt like a normal kid. I got to play and be silly with my brothers. We weren't well liked in our neighborhood and all the kids always wanted to fight us. And they always got that fight. We had no rules to follow, and often stayed out well past dark. But spending the morning jumping and having fun was so much more fun.

Later that afternoon, Miss Chimney and Miss Jennifer came over with birthday cupcakes for Tim's birthday. They seemed nervous, but I didn't care because we had cupcakes. I took mine outside and continued to play. As I was enjoying myself, the feeling of guilt hit me. How could I be so happy with this stranger? What about my mom? What would she do? Would I ever see her again? All of these questions and emotions ruined the sunshine and all I wanted to do was sleep it away. Even in all of this mess, at least my siblings and I are all together because they are all I have. The hours turned into days and those turned into weeks. Miss Jennifer had visited several times and told us that our mom had classes to do before we could see her again. So, we waited and continued to enjoy regular life. Although I liked my new life, my heart yearned for my mom.

4

Child Haven, Not Heaven

It was now July and I was looking forward to my eighth birthday. One day I was in the living room watching cartoons when someone knocked on the door. Miss Caroline opened it to see Miss Jennifer standing there along with another woman. I turned my attention from the television to the door. Miss Caroline let them in and told us all to join her in the dining room. Once there Miss Jennifer told us that we were all going to a children's home until my mother was ready to take us back. I looked at Miss Caroline who would not make eye contact with me. I asked Miss Jennifer why we couldn't just wait here with Miss Caroline? She bent over and wiped the tears that had started coming down my cheeks. She told me that Miss Caroline can only be a temporary foster parent. I did not understand this at all! Why wasn't my mom done with her class? My fear turned to anger when Miss Jennifer and the other lady went to gather all our things. I never got to say goodbye to Miss Caroline, nor did I ever see her again. We all got into a large white van, the kind that can seat 15 people. Jatia and I sat in the front row while AD and Tim sat in the last row. We drove through our neighborhood, Muskegon Heights and went towards downtown.

The words "Child Haven" were posted in front of a large brown brick building. It kind of looked like a mini prison. My siblings and I entered the building hand in hand with Jatia leading us. Once inside the place, I noticed huge playroom filled with any toy you might want to play with along with the new PlayStation gaming console. My anger started to subside when I saw all the amazing toys waiting for me.

There was a black woman inside the office which was near the playroom. She introduced herself as Miss Lynn and told us she was the manager of the home. I looked out the glass windows that surrounded the office and there were kids everywhere. Most were black with a few Hispanic kids as well. Miss Lynn told us we could join the other kids in the playroom, then she closed the door to speak with Miss Jennifer. My siblings and I found a spot on a sofa in front of the television where we stayed until Miss Jennifer came back. When she did, she told us that we were going to stay here until my mom gets a chance to talk to the judge. After that she left without another word. We stayed on that sofa until Miss Lynn told us it was time for bed.

After a while, Child Haven didn't seem too bad. It was summertime so every day the staff took us on some type of field trip. On one trip, one of the workers took every child she had in her van to see their parents. We had about fifteen people in our van, so before we left she made us all promise that we wouldn't tell anyone. That day everyone got to see their family except us. As usual, our mom wasn't home. It was then that I lost all hope in my mother. When we returned to Child Haven, Miss Lynn told us that Miss Jennifer had stopped by to tell us that we would get to see our mother soon. For a moment I got excited, but then I remembered that mom hadn't shown up earlier and my eagerness subsided.

Days later, we got a call from Miss Jennifer telling us we would get to see our mother that afternoon. I got a nervous feeling that made my stomach ache. I liked this place. We got to eat every day and there were toys. I don't want to have to get up at the crack of dawn anymore to collect cans for food.

But, I do miss my mom and it would be nice to see her. That afternoon I got dressed in my best outfit. Jatia, Tim, Alex and I all eagerly waited for Miss Jennifer to get there.

She pulled up in an off-grey, Pontiac Grand Am. I was thankful it wasn't a police car again. I couldn't breathe the last time. My brothers and I piled into the back while Jatia accompanied Miss Jennifer in the front. We drove a short way and pulled into the parking lot of the Catholic Social Services Building on Apple Street. Once inside, Miss Jennifer showed us to a room with a dirty looking old couch with a lot of baby toys on it. We all sat down and quietly waited for our mom to come in. There was a clock on the wall. It said 2:44 p.m. The visit was scheduled to start at 3 p.m. The feeling in my stomach came back. It stayed that way for the next three hours. At 6:00 p.m., Miss Jennifer piled us back into her car. Our mother never came.

On the ride back to Child Haven, Miss Jennifer told us we would be leaving Child Haven soon to go to a foster home. I asked her why we couldn't stay where we were? And she said it was only for temporary placement.

That night I lay awake in bed, imagining my siblings and I in a huge house with a white picket fence laughing. I guess I had been dreaming because the laughing in my mind turned into real-life screaming as I opened my eyes. Jatia was in the hall screaming at the top of her lungs! I jumped out of bed to see what was going on. When I opened the door, I saw Miss Jennifer kneeling down next to Jatia trying to calm her down. When Miss Jennifer saw me in the hallway, she told me to collect my things. I went back into the room and looked around. This room had become my room. I had my paintings and pictures tacked on the wall. For the second time, I had to pack everything in the navy-blue, hard suitcase Miss Caroline had given me.

When I got to the front door all my siblings were already there with their things. There was another woman with Miss Jennifer who I didn't know. Miss Jennifer came over and told Jatia and I that we were going to a foster home to live with the Beasleys. The other lady then began to take Tim and Alex with her. I violently took my hand from her and asked her where my brothers were going. She got down to my level and told me that there wasn't a foster home that could take all four of us. So, until my mom got done with her court orders we would be in separate homes. I had never been away from my big brothers. I was scared and went to hide under the table in the hallway. Sometime later, Jatia came over and brought me from under the table. Hand in hand, we left Child Haven not knowing what was waiting ahead of us.

5

Beasts or Beasleys

At first, the Beasleys were very nice people. They had four children - three of whom were also foster kids. The two oldest, Juan and Tony, were about fifteen or sixteen years old. The Beasley's real son, Anton, was seven years old, my age. The youngest was a little girl who looked to be around four years old. After Miss Jennifer introduced us to the family, she asked if we were ok. And without waiting for an answer, she was out the door. Jatia and I just stood there looking at this wealthy black family. This was something we had never seen before. How could they take care of so many children and live in such a nice house?

Mrs. Beasley asked if she could show us to our room. And she told us to call her Patty. She was a heavyset black woman maybe in her mid-forties. She had on a pair of leopard print tights with a matching top. She wore rings on all of her fingers and had about the same amount of gold chains around her neck. She had a short afro and smelled of strong perfume.

She took us up a staircase that was in the kitchen. The first thing I noticed was the ceiling upstairs. It had a texture that looked like popcorn with glitter in it. The rest of the house was decorated nicely as well with black leather couches and golden, mirrored coffee tables. They had a big screen television and an entertainment system complete with a VHS recorder. I had never seen such a nice house before. I asked myself, why would she let strangers live here in this nice house?

Once upstairs, she told us that we would be sleeping in the same room. I was happy that I would be close to my sister. She showed us our room which was smaller than the room we had at our mom's house. All it had room for was a large dresser and bunk beds. On the way back to the kitchen I saw three other rooms that looked very nice. I asked Patty if those were the other kids' rooms. She looked at me and laughed. She said that those niggas would tear her house up, so they sleep in the basement where the playroom was located. I then asked what the rooms were used for? She responded that it was her house to do as she pleased and scorned me. I got the feeling that she didn't want me asking any more questions. Once back into the kitchen, she went over some house rules, which included not going into the nice rooms. Patty told us that we were free to go outside any time and into the basement. That's it. She told us that we were not allowed in any other bedroom in the house including Anton's and the little girl's room. The whole time, Jatia and I just sat there listening, not saying a word. Patty told us that they were frying fish for dinner, so until it is done we should go downstairs in the basement with the other kids.

Her basement was not like the rest of her house. It was a normal, unfinished Michigan basement that was cold, dark and damp. There were cement floors with pipes overhead and the support beams that held up the house. I saw an old box TV with a raggedy torn sofa that Juan and Tony were sitting on. They were watching Dragon Ball Z and looked up when they saw Jatia and I. They didn't speak to me but were really friendly to my sister. They asked her what our mom had done. Jatia did not share their friendliness and guided me towards the television to watch it. Seeing that my sister was ignoring them, Juan and Tony went to their room. It wasn't more than a couple of pieces of plywood all nailed together to make a makeshift partition in the basement.

Later that evening, we had Bluegill fish for dinner, which was my first time eating that type of fish. When I bit into the fish my mouth was welcomed by knifelike bones, naturally I screamed out in pain while the other kids laughed at me. After dinner, Jatia and I were told to do the dishes, then head to bed.

That night I laid awake coming up with different scenarios for my future. I started to feel guilty for not missing my mom's house, but I was glad to get out of there. I was so tired of the midnight meetings and the beatings. With all those thoughts swimming around my head, I began drifting off to sleep watching the sparkly specks in the ceiling reflect the light from the nightlight.

The next morning, Mrs. Beasley knocked on the door around 7 a.m. I was already up. I was too nervous to go downstairs without my sister. Jatia and I got dressed and went to the kitchen. The aroma in there was to die for! Mrs. Patty had made pancakes, bacon, and hash browns with all the fixings. I just stood there eyeing the food like it was going to disappear. Mrs. Patty told Jatia and I to grab a bowl of cereal and not to touch the other food. She told us we could have two bowls if we wanted because we had a lot of work to do. Mr. Beasley, the little girl, and Anton all made plates with the feast on the stove and sat in the formal dining room.

At the breakfast table in the kitchen, where the foster kids ate, Jatia asked Juan what Mrs. Beasley meant about having work to do. He told us that the Beasleys owned an ice cream shop and they helped run it. Jatia asked if they got paid and how many days a week we were expected to help out. Juan snickered a little and told us that they had to work six days a week. And since it's summertime, he said they are usually there all day. As for the pay, he said Mrs. Patty says they have to earn their keep. I was really excited because helping at an ice cream shop sounded really fun.

We all piled into the Beasley's Suburban SUV and headed to their shop. When we got there, it was not what I had in mind. I was expecting a place with a playground and bright colored pictures of the ice cream TV characters. It was the complete opposite! It was a very small, old building with chipped paint. There was a field that could have served as a nice playground, but it was overflowing with weeds. They did have a basketball hoop in the parking lot that was rusted and on its last leg. Juan and Tony jumped out of the truck and started right to work, getting the place ready to open. I was also excited to help and asked Mrs. Beasley what I could do. She handed Jatia and I gloves and told us that she wanted the field beside the shop to be free of weeds by the end of the day. My excitement subsided very quickly once I saw how much work we had to do.

It took us all morning and most of the afternoon to clear the lot. Along with ice cream, the shop also sold a Detroit favorite called a "walking taco." It's a taco inside of a fifty cents Doritos bag. You put ground beef, cheese, salsa and all of the other toppings in the Dorito bag shake it up and eat it. I figured that we would be able to choose something off the menu, seeing that we had earned our share. I was dumbfounded when Mrs. Patty handed us a can of Vienna sausages. To add insult to injury, she made a remark about being happy that we were even eating. Jatia and I took our sausages and sat under the tree at the picnic table. As we were sitting at the table, I saw Anton walking up to us with a huge cheesy pile of nachos. Juan and Tony also got sausages, so I assumed that only the family could eat at the shop because it was their family business. Still I got jealous as he sat across from me smacking down on the nachos, chewing with his mouth open. I quickly finished my meal and got up from the table. I went to see what else Mrs. Patty wanted me to do. As I walked up to her, she and her husband were closing the shop. She told me to take the trash out and stay outside with the other kids until they were done. The trash was really gross but sweet smelling from the ice cream and other sweets that were thrown out. I took the bag to the trash can and when I lifted the lid, I saw Anton's nachos sitting in the can half-eaten.

My stomach growled as we waited for the Beasleys to finish closing up the shop. We got back to their house around 8 p.m., and Mrs. Patty told us to shower then come down for dinner. As usual, I showered with my sister and got dressed for bed. As I made my way to the kitchen, I saw Mrs. Patty at the front door exchanging money for a pizza. I became very excited, still starving from all the work I had done earlier that day. When I entered the kitchen, sitting on the counter was the ingredients to make ham sandwiches for the foster kids with Capri-Sun juices beside them. For us, the four foster kids, we never saw the pizza. It was for the family only.

6

Down by the Lake

Every day was the same routine - get up, work, barely eat then repeat. I began hating the summer. Oh, how I counted down the days. So much has happened in three months. By the end of the summer I was so overworked and so hungry I could barely stand It. All I could do was look forward to the school year to start. I had no idea where I would attend school for my third grade year, but where didn't matter, as long as would I get to go. We were taken a month before my seventh birthday in July, so clearly I would not be attending Roosevelt Elementary again.

The last week of summer, Mr. Beasley informed us that we would be going on a fishing trip on his boat. Seeing that Mrs. Patty was very afraid of the water and was often very seasick, she opted to stay home with the two youngest and allowed all the foster kids to go.

The drive to the lake took about an hour. During the entire time, Juan and Tony kept touching Jatia in between her legs. When we arrived at the lake, Mr. Beasley backed the small fishing boat into the water while Juan "helped" Jatia into the boat. Once we were all in, Mr. Beasley started the pull engine and we were off. I must admit even though I hated the Beasleys and that house, in this moment I was at peace and content. The sound of the motor muted everything in the real world even my thoughts. The orange-red, Michigan, evening sun kissed my cheeks with a mother's touch. Then, as sudden as this euphoria had come upon me, it was gone with the turn of the ignition.

I have never liked fishing because it required touching gross, dead insects and fish. So, I sat back and watched while the others fished. Jatia, Juan and Tony were on one side of the boat while Mr. Beasley was on the other. I sat towards the front of the boat looking into the cold clear water. I looked up when I heard water dripping and saw that it was Juan pissing off the boat with his penis right by Jatia's face. Tony chuckled, stood up and proceeded to do the same. Mr. Beasley looked over his shoulder at them and turned back to his rod. The only thing that kept me from jumping up and pushing Juan off that boat was the fact that Jatia laughed. She seemed to enjoy it in some disgusting manner. Even at my young age, I realized that my sister wasn't the average girl. She never wore girly clothes likes skirts or dresses. Her beautiful long black hair is always either in cornrows or in tight ponytails. She did nothing to show her girly side. And because of that most of the boys in our neighborhood thought of her as one of the boys instead of one of the girls they chased. So, getting this attention from them was new to her.

It made my blood boil as I saw them disrespect my sister. For the rest of time we were on the water, I stared into the clear blue Lake Michigan water. As we made our way back to the shore, the burnt orange summer sun was putting itself out on the lake horizon. In that moment, I felt at peace and happy again. This realization made me more upset. How could I feel anything but pain? I have been taken away from everything I have ever known. And to make it worst, my sister was starting to act strange towards me. She was always my protector and provider but now she was distant and rarely spoke to me. If it wasn't clear that Jatia liked the attention on the boat, she made it blatantly apparent in the truck. Instead of sitting with me in the back, she sat between Juan and Tony. We finally got back to the Beasley house. And instead of coming upstairs and helping me get ready for bed like she always did, Jatia went downstairs to the cold, dark foster child prison basement.

7

The Fight That Changed My Life

Jatia became more and more distant as the week went on. One morning, the weekend before school started, Jatia showed her ultimate betrayal. I was outside on the sidewalk using the bike that Anton and I shared. I guess Anton was tired of me riding the bike and went and told Juan that I threatened him. Juan came outside and told me to get off the bike. I simply refused because the day before Anton had the bike the entire day! As I was telling Juan this, Anton came over and picked me up and threw me onto the ground. Anton grabbed the bike and eagerly mounted it. I got up, not even noticing the scrapes on my knees and elbows. As Anton began to ride away, I lunged at him with all my might and tackled him to the ground. Everyone in the house heard the commotion and made their way to the front yard.

Before when we lived with momma, if one of us got into a fight, momma expected us all to help out. We all have been fighting since we climbed out of the womb it seems. I remember this one time. My brother, Tim, got into a fight over *Pokemon* cards with the kid that lived across the street. But, on this particular day, the neighbor kid grabbed a bat after losing to Tim. When I saw him take out the bat, I proceeded to run into the house and grab butcher knives. I made my way back to the street and brandished my weapons daring him to approach my siblings and I. The police ended up being called and we all ran inside.

As I was there fighting Anton and Juan, I was handling myself well for an eight-year-old. But they eventually got me to the ground and that's when all hell broke loose. One pinned me down while the other two kicked blows into my head and torso. This lasted for what seemed like a thousand hours but was cut short due to an elderly neighbor who had called the police. As the police arrived, Mrs. Beasley told all the kids including Jatia to go inside. The police officer came over and helped me to his car, while another one confronted the Beasleys. From the crack in the window of the officer's car, I heard Mrs. Beasley yelling and telling them that I had tried to kill her sons and that I was dangerous. She told them, "that nigger is not welcome in my house." The police asked for my case worker's information and thanked the Beasleys. They both walked back to the car with looks of annoyance on their faces - as if they were tired of dealing with ghetto black kids. But when they got back into the car, they called Miss Jennifer who wasn't answering because it was a Saturday. They told me that I would have to go back to Child Haven until Monday.

So, we made our way through familiar streets until the car came to a stop in front of Child Haven. I hated Child Haven. It was anything but a haven for children. It was gross, from the old spider webs in the corner to the "food" they fed you. It wasn't so bad the last time I was here. I guess it was because I at least had the comfort of my siblings. This was the very first time I was completely alone. I had never cried so hard before in my life. The cry that hurts your gut and tires you out. For the first seven years of my life and being the youngest, I've never been alone. I have shared everything from beds to baths with my siblings. Now, I am alone.

Aloneness, it is something that simply cannot be shared. Child Haven was the lair for aloneness.

Not having my siblings there made it even harder since no one liked me because they said that I had sugar in the tank. I never really knew what that meant but I knew that it was not a good thing. The first time I heard that phrase one of my mom's many boyfriends found me and my friend Jamal behind the garage. I was showing him what my mom's old boyfriend used to make me do. I was interested to see if I felt the same way if it was my choice instead of it happening to me. He yelled at me and told my mom that I had sugar in my tank. Ever since that day I have been called that and much worse but I always had my big brothers and my sister to have my back.

After that first night back in Child Haven, I became very isolated. The other boys didn't like me and I wasn't allowed to play with the girls. Jatia and I have always had a close relationship. But after what happened recently, I was rude and mean to the girls. It had been weeks since I had seen or heard from my siblings. My mom had canceled the latest visit, so I didn't even get to see her there. On the ride back to the haven, Jennifer told me that they still hadn't found a home for me, but she was working on it. I felt exhausted, physically and mentally. I hated myself because I had done this to myself. I drove my mother away and then Jatia. I wanted nothing to do with myself. When we parked in front of the Haven, I jumped out of the car and I ran towards a busy intersection. I cannot honestly share with you what was going through my mind because it was blank. Blank as a screen on a word document, and the little black indicator was my heartbeat. On beat, peaceful yet demanding and unyielding. I threw myself in front of a white van and hoped for the worst.

For some reason the universe was not ready to let me leave. The van braked and avoided me, just barely causing a head-on collision. Miss Jennifer got to me and asked me if I was ok. I told her "no, I wanted to die." I want to leave this empty feeling and the only way I thought was to leave the earth. She then when to the drivers and apologized while a Child Haven employee put me back into her car. Miss Jennifer came back to the car and made a phone call. She talked for about ten minutes and the conversation was muffled due to the heavy traffic nearby. Miss Jennifer got back into the car after she got off the phone. She didn't have her usual smile planted on her face, instead she looked scared. She told me that she was going to take me to talk to my therapist, Eric, so I could tell him how I was feeling.

It was pretty late when we made it to community health. Eric was outside the building, which otherwise looked empty. I had been here many times, four times a month to be exact. All the siblings and I were enrolled in therapy when we were first taken into foster care. I didn't mind the toys they had in the waiting room, but I always got a creepy feeling with Eric. He was very tall and skinny and always wore the ugliest ties. He wore the thickest reading glasses I've ever seen and always smelled of coffee. He was his usual self this time as well. Miss Jennifer led me into the building and told me to go to the kid's corner to play with the toys. It seemed like we had been there for hours as I played with the coloring books. Miss Jennifer and Eric stood by the door talking softly, but I couldn't determine what they were talking about. All of a sudden, I looked up from my coloring book and I saw an ambulance pull in front of the building next to Miss Jennifer's car. The paramedics pulled the stretcher out of the back of the truck and made their way toward the door. Jennifer came over to the window that I was looking out and told me that Eric couldn't treat me here anymore and that I would have to see a new doctor. I didn't mind that at all, but I didn't understand why I had to go in an ambulance. The paramedics were talking to Eric when Miss Jennifer walked me to the door. They lowered they stretcher and asked if I could lie down. I did what they asked not wanting to get into trouble. When I laid down, I was strapped onto the thing by my legs and arms, which freaked the hell out of me. I started fighting and crying. I looked at Miss Jennifer and even she had tears boiling in her eyes. She told me to calm down and to let the paramedics do their job. They loaded me into the ambulance. And Miss Jennifer told me not to worry because she would be right behind me. They closed the doors, and off I went to my unknown location.

8

Straitjackets and Soft Rooms

When the ambulance stopped, the doors opened and the paramedic that had been riding in the ambulance with me, hopped out and began to take the stretcher out. Once outside, they did not unstrap me. Instead, they wheeled the stretcher into the big brick building with small barred windows. Miss Jennifer met us at the door. And when it opened a very tall man in white scrubs handed Jennifer a clipboard and began unstrapping me. The relief I felt was short-lived, as the nurse crossed my arms and put me into a straitjacket. I had never even seen a straitjacket in real life, nonetheless, imagine myself in one. I wish I could describe the feeling I had at that moment. But even now, like then, the way I felt was descriptive-less.

We made our way through a labyrinth of halls. The sounds coming from behind the doors we passed were traumatizing. Miss Jennifer seemed to be talking to me, but I was numb. Every part of my body was numb. We stopped at a door that was to my right. It had a small window that seemed to be tempered. By this time, Miss Jennifer had completed the paperwork the nurse had given her. She turned to me and told me that everything will be ok. The nurse opened the door and asked me to enter. The room was pretty bare, only having what you can loosely call a bed that held a thin, flimsy mattress. The barred windows that I had seen outside were in this room as well. There was also a small bathroom attached to my room. It was very similar to the bathrooms that you find in hospital rooms with the large low toilets and walk-in showers with a resting stool. As I walked through the door, the it closed behind me. I instantly lost it. Looking back at it now, they probably thought I was a nutcase. By that time, I had had enough. I had lost everything that I had ever known. My home, school, friends, and family were all gone.

Defeated, I climbed onto the thin mattress. Numb and done with life, I fell asleep that first night at Pine Rest Mental Hospital. I was jolted awake to the morning light peering through my barred windows. Someone in the hallways was screaming at the top of their lungs. Oddly, the voice sounded like a man's voice, not a boy's. I stuck my head out of my door to see what was going on and I saw a grown man in a diaper. He was digging shit out of it and throwing it while screaming at the nurses. Disgusted, I closed my door, and started dry heaving. I sat on the bed, looking at the four empty walls that were surrounding me. They had no personality, no emotions, no life. For some reason, I felt safe within these walls because I understood its aloneness.

Suddenly, there was a knock at my door. A female nurse stuck her head into my room and told me that it was time for breakfast. I sat there for a few short moments and then got up and walked down the hall. There was a line of people who seem to be waiting for a tray ,so I got in line as well. Like last night, there were adults in line, but this time there was kids as well. All of these people were really weird to me. Most people were making noises and some were even drooling on themselves. The line moved closer to the half door that was open. When it was my turn, the nurse in the little room handed me a small container with five pills with a small Dixie cup with water in it. Without hesitating, I threw the pills in my mouth just like all the others had done before me. The nurse asked me to open my mouth and stick out my tongue. After I had done that, she handed me my tray and sent me down the hall.

In the cafeteria, there were about six large round tables with a buffet table at the back of the room. It wasn't much of a buffet. There was cereal, milk, soft apples, and a sad excuse for orange juice. I got myself a bowl of Fruit Loops and sat at a table by myself. Others started sitting at the table with me including the grown man in the diapers I had seen when I arrived last night.

Honestly, to this day, my first couple of days in Pine Rest Mental Hospital were blurry. They kept us on a very repetitive schedule. I found myself looking forward to receiving my daily cocktail of meds. They made my mind stop running. I finally felt content but at the same time my body started going through weird changes. In the weeks I was at Pine Rest, I had gained quite a bit of weight and my mood swings were less often but more violent when they occurred.

One of the few memories I have from Pine Rest is playing outside in the sun. It felt amazing. Although we were outside, we were still confined within a 20-foot-tall wooden fence. It was a prison, but they kept me so drugged up that I couldn't feel my despair. I soon started hiding my pills under my tongue. I wanted my mind back. I wanted to think clearly. I needed to figure a way to get out of that place! I soon stopped going into the playroom with the other patients, and mostly stayed in my room. I partially did this, so the staff didn't notice that I wasn't a zombie like the others.

I remember one time sitting in my room and looking out of the window thinking about what I wanted to do when I grew up. I decided that no matter what, I wanted to be the voice for all of those who were in my situation.

Days turned into weeks and those turned into about two months before I heard from Miss Jennifer again. She told me that she had found me a home with no other children and it was in Whitehall, Michigan, a quiet, small wooded community. I didn't care where I went as long as it wasn't Pine Rest or Child Haven.

9

Into the Woods

A couple days later I was in the backseat of Miss Jennifer's Pontiac Grand Am. I was so relieved not to be in that mental hospital anymore. And I made the decision right then and there that I would never say or do anything that could possibly put me in that place again. We drove for what felt like forever. Miss Jennifer told me that there was a home for me in Whitehall, Michigan, and that there weren't any other kids placed there so the foster parent could work with me and my issues.

I had never been out of the city of Muskegon, so going to a home in the woods was all new for me. As we drove down wooded roads, I noticed horse farms and a lot of Christmas tree farms as well. We finally turned into a driveway of a small cottage-looking house with an elderly black woman waiting at the end of the driveway. Miss Jennifer got me out of the car and introduced me to the woman. She said her name was Ms. Jones and that she was happy to have me stay with her. She had greying black hair that was slicked into a ponytail. She told me that she liked to be outdoors either hunting or fishing. Ms. Jones showed me around the small house, which wasn't more than two rooms and a kitchen. My room was in the back of the house, next to a very small restroom. Miss Jennifer and Ms. Jones spoke in the hallway while I got settled into my room. I could hear Miss Jennifer explaining how and when to give me my prescription meds. Miss Jennifer then came into my room and told me to be good, and that she would see me soon for our sibling visit. And just like that she was in her car pulling out of the driveway.

After the day I had, I desperately needed a long hot bath. I went into the bathroom and began to run water for a bath. At first the water was clear like any other bath, but after a moment it began to come out rusty looking and smelled of eggs. What the fuck was this!? I went out into the small cottage kitchen and I asked Ms. Jones about the water. She told me because the house was situated on a well sometimes the water comes out with iron and other minerals in it. Needless to say, I skipped bathing and joined Ms. Jones in the living room. She had two reclining chairs and a small TV. She was watching *Touched By An Angel*. Ms. Jones was nice enough I told myself. I was actually glad that I was the only foster child in the home with her. It was the first time ever in my life where I was the only kid. I must have drifted off to sleep. Ms. Jones woke me up. I had fallen asleep on the chair, and she told me to head to bed.

Living in the country was a huge change for me. I had never lived in the woods before. At first, I loved it. I loved the space I could just run around in Ms. Jones' huge yard. And this was the first time I could ride a bike in the street and not have to worry about cars. I started to get comfortable with living with her. She worked at the Ford Factory and was really never home.

I soon started school at Whitehall Elementary, and it was the nicest school I had ever seen. Everything in it looked new, even the books looked brand new. During my first day, I met Cody. He seemed kind of spoiled but literally was the only one at school that spoke to me that first day. As I was going through my day, I noticed that I was one of the only black students there.

My teacher was hearing impaired, but all of the students knew how to sign with her. I knew what they were doing because in Muskegon I remembered learning how to sign the alphabet. She let me know that she could read my lips. She also told me that I would pick up how to use sign language very easily. Class was okay and soon the bell rang for lunch. I walked into the lunchroom feeling completely alone. I got my lunch tray and found a spot at the end of a table that was mostly empty. I can see the other kids pointing at me, but I told myself to ignore them. This was the first time that I had gone to a nice school and been enrolled in normal classes. I was always in special education classes when I lived with my mom. It was partially because of my behavior and because my mom kept me in these classes so I could get more behavioral drugs that my mom sold. As I was eating my lunch, a little white girl with blond hair walked over to me. At first, I was excited, but then she asked if it was true that I was a foster child. I shrugged my shoulders. Then, she asked me if I was slow or something and walked away laughing. I felt like an outsider and anger boiled inside of me. Going to an inner city school, there were more kids that looked like me and came from a similar home situation. At this school everyone seemed so different. I finished my lunch and headed outside for recess. Recess was no better. Nobody played with me, so I just swung on the swing in the corner.

10

Crushing on Cody

The rest of my first day was okay. I felt really isolated and alone, but I was still happy to be at a new school. The school bus pulled up to Ms. Jones' street and I thought I was the only kid that lived on that road. But, to my surprise, a kid who I had seen in my class also got off at my bus stop. We both started walking down the road and he asked me if I had a good first day. I lied and told him, yeah, but I think he knew that I wasn't telling the truth. And would you believe it was Cody? He asked me if I would like to be friends. I said yes. Then, he asked where I lived. I told him where I lived. He then pointed to a huge house with horses out front that was a little ways down the road from Ms. Jones' house. I told him I would see him tomorrow and headed into the house.

Cody ended up being my best friend at White Hall elementary. Eventually, I started going over to his house and playing video games with him. And his mom even taught me how to horseback ride. It was a blast. If I am honest, Cody was the first boy I thought was cute. He had bleach blond hair with stunning blue eyes. To me, the most attractive thing about him was his personality. Since the first day of school, he did not care that I was different or in foster care. He seemed to like me for me.

The next few weeks in White Hall was amazing. I began to hang out with Cody every day after school and even joined his baseball little league. Ms. Jones was always working, so things at home were pretty good as well. I couldn't remember a time when I didn't have to worry, I had plenty of food. Even though most kids were still being mean, my school was tolerable, especially having Cody at my side. To me, my life couldn't get any better.

One day after school, I came home to see Ms. Jones sitting in the small kitchen at the table. She was crying and really upset. I asked her what was going on. The oh so similar feeling started to creep down my throat creating a knot in my stomach. I thought my perfect little world was about to come to an end. But to my surprise, it had nothing to do with me. Ms. Jones told me that her daughter had died, and we would have to go Detroit for her funeral and to bury her.

11

Heading to the Funeral

I had seen old photos around the house of Ms. Jones and a little girl. But by now, I had learned not to ask foster parents about their children. She had never shared anything about her with me. And I had never heard her speaking to anyone about her. I was excited to go to Detroit! Miss Jennifer had told me that my mother moved there and I knew a lot of my family lived there. It was my hope to run into one of them while there. Maybe I will get some answers as to why my mom had not been to visit with us in a while.

That weekend we packed Ms. Jones red Ford F250 and hit the highway. It was a four hour drive to Detroit, and Ms. Jones played old school R&B the entire trip. We arrived right before nightfall and pulled up to a pretty, two-story brick home. Ms. Jones and I got out of the truck and were greeted by laughter and hellos from her family. There was an older black man that helped me with the bags and showed me to my room. I settled down and got myself ready for bed. I was exhausted and I was praying that I might see one of my family members. I drifted off to sleep - peaceful and hopeful.

The next morning, there was a huge breakfast and lots of people in the house. I mainly kept to myself listening to old family stories. Ms. Jones seemed very happy with her family. She was usually quiet and tired but here she was way different. She even bragged about me and said I was a good foster child. I felt really proud of myself.

As I was sitting there listening, I started to remember the last time I was in Detroit with my mom, my three siblings, and my uncle. I remember we were at my grandma's apartment. My mom got into an argument with a guy because he was sitting on her car which was parked in front of the building. The guy told my mom that she was in enemy territory and to watch her back. Unbothered by their threats, my mom rolled her eyes. We went up to my grandma's apartment and had dinner. My mom told us we were going to Diary Queen for dessert, and we went downstairs to get into the car. All of a sudden a group of four men came from around the other side of the building and started fighting my mom and my Uncle Feeky. Without hesitation, Jatia jumped into the fight and Alex, Tim, and I followed. I was really young and small. I couldn't really do anything, but I wanted to help my family. So, I did the only thing that I could think of doing. I bit the men on their ankles and legs. My mom and uncle along with the rest of us beat the men up and won the fight. I remember how my mom bragged about how "gangster" her kids were and how proud she was of us. That was the last time I felt proud.

But the proudness that Ms. Jones said about me wasn't about fighting or anything violent. She seemed happy that I was just enjoying my life and following the rules. This was the first time that I felt proud of being good.

The funeral came and went without any incidents. I had never seen a dead person or been to a funeral so I was very intrigued by it all. At the burial when the coffin was being lowered, I remembered thinking how final death was. I was scared of death. The aloneness of it all and knowing that my family might not even know if I was dead or not.

It was Sunday night and the last night in Detroit. My hopes of running into my family started to fade. I was in the kitchen waiting for dinner to be finished when I saw someone's cellphone on the counter. I had memorized Jatia's phone number and I desperately wanted to talk to her. I took the phone and went to my room. Back in the day before our current fancy iPhones with passcodes, cell phones were unprotected and very easy to use. I flipped open the phone and dialed my sister's number. It rang and rang, then went to voicemail. I called several times with no success. I decided that it was too risky to keep the phone for the night and decided to put the phone back on the counter. When I got to the kitchen the owner of the phone was already looking for it. I tried to sneak it back on the counter, hoping that no one would see me. But I was caught by Ms. Jones. She asked me why I took their phone. I just stood there and shrugged my shoulders indicating I didn't know why. She told me to go to my room and to not come down until she was ready to leave.

I went to the room feeling so guilty about what I had done. They thought I was going to try to steal the cellphone but that wasn't my intention at all. Seeing Ms. Jones with her family over the weekend made me sad and miss my family. I heard voices from downstairs coming though the floor vent and to my surprise I heard a phone ring and the man answering the phone. He asked who this was and said that he didn't know any Jatia. I didn't leave a voicemail so my sister would not have known it was me who had called her. The man hung up the phone and I immediately felt at ease. I was happy though that my sister called back and that the number I had for her still worked.

We piled into the small truck the next morning and headed back to Whitehall. I didn't get the chance to see or talk to my family, but I still had hope. I don't remember much of the drive home since I was dozing off to sleep. I awoke as we made our way down our dark country street. I went to my room exhausted and excited to go back to school.

12

Thankful for a Break

The next morning, I met Cody at the bus stop and got back into my routine. Over the next several weeks, I spent a lot of time at Cody's house playing *Super Mario* on his Nintendo. His mom drove us to our baseball practices and always picked me up for the games every Saturday. School was getting better because I had my best friend Cody even though some of the kids still taunted me. But I wasn't going to let that get me down.

The leaves on the trees start to change as fall drew closer. A few days before Thanksgiving, Ms. Jones told me that she would be going out of state to visit family for Thanksgiving and that I would go to a respite home for a week. I had heard of respite homes from others kids when I was at Child Haven. Respite homes are temporary foster homes that you go to when your regular foster parent needs a break or goes on vacation. This made me very upset not only because I couldn't hang out with Cody during winter break, but I was going to spend my Thanksgiving with complete strangers. I started to become passive aggressive as Thanksgiving drew closer, and Ms. Jones was constantly yelling at me.

Miss Jennifer came to my school the day before winter break and picked me up to take me to my temporary foster home. She talked to my teacher who let her know that I was doing very well and getting settled into the school. I still had a chip on my shoulder but I wondered what type of family I would be staying with. It had been months since I was placed with Ms. Jones and that had began to feel like my home.

As Miss Jennifer was driving, it started to snow. The trees were so beautiful with all of the fall colored leaves that were being covered with snow. Even as an adult today, the first snow in the fall is my favorite thing. We drove for about twenty minutes before Jennifer pulled into a long driveway. At the end of the driveway was a huge modern looking house with a black Range Rover in the driveway. Ms. Jones had put my clothes into a black garbage bag that I retrieved out of the trunk. Miss Jennifer stood with me at the front door as she rang the doorbell. I heard dogs barking and footsteps make their way to the door. When the door opened a really pretty, white lady with blond hair and a comforting smile greeted us. There was a beautiful golden retriever at her feet wagging its tail in excitement. She kneeled down and introduced herself as Lindsey and told me that her husband Gary and her were excited to watch me for the week. Miss Jennifer gave her my meds and the dosing instructions. Then, she told me to be good and that she would see me in a week. Soon thereafter, she was out the door and backing her car down the driveway. Lindsey stood at the door with me and waved until Miss Jennifer was out of sight. Then, she asked me if I wanted to see my room. I shook my head yes and we made our way through the house. The house was so nice and modern. It even smelled like fresh paint. There was a huge big screen TV in the living room with a large leather couch. The dog trailed behind us occasionally sniffing me, which I did not like.

Growing up, I was taught to be afraid of dogs especially big ones. The dogs in the hood were always mean and I had been bitten before, so I watched him with caution. I remember the day I got bitten like it was yesterday. I was riding my bike and looking for pop cans to turn in for cash when a large Rottweiler jumped a fence and chased me. I lost control, fell off my bike and the dog bit my leg. Screaming, I used my bike to hit the dog and he let go. I asked Lindsey if he would bite me and she assured me that he wouldn't. She told me that the dog's name was Gus and he was fourteen years old. As we passed the kitchen, she went into the pantry and got a treat for Gus and told me to give it to him. I held it in my hand waiting to pull my hand back if he tried to bite me, but he didn't. He took the treat and went on his way.

After showing me the house, we went upstairs to see the room I would be staying in. When Lindsey opened the door, I immediately got super excited! There was so many toys in the room. There was even a large Lego table with a bunch of Legos on it. I asked her if there were other children here and her smile faded. She told me that this used to be Brian's room, her foster son, who she and her husband were hoping to adopt. But his mother had recently completed parenting classes and got custody of him again. I can tell that she was getting sad, so I quickly switched the subject by asking her what we were having for dinner. She told me that her husband Gary was going to pick up pizza on his way home.

I was in the room I was staying in and playing with the toys when her husband arrived with the pizza. Lindsey came up to my room and let me know that dinner was ready. When I went into the kitchen her husband Gary was there and he looked just as perfect as Lindsey. He had bright blue eyes and perfectly manicured blond hair that was combed over. They seemed to be the perfect couple in a perfect house. He greeted me with a smile and asked if I was hungry. I told him yes and he put a couple of pizza slices on a plate for me. I sat down at the kitchen table and began to eat when Lindsey invited me to eat in the living room so we could watch tv as well. I grabbed my plate and made my way into the living room. I remember Lindsey turning on a concert and there were three white woman with blond hair singing country music. She asked me if I had ever heard of the "Dixie

Chicks." I told her I had not. She went on and on about the band and how she had seen them live and whatnot. I felt really comfortable here. I'm not sure if it was because of how perfect they seemed to be or how interactive Lindsey was with me. I told myself that I would love parents like them.

I finished my pizza and Lindsey tucked me into bed and read me a book. I had never had anyone read to me before bed. I had seen it happen in the movies, but it had never happened to me in real life. I fell asleep before the end of the story, content with my new surroundings. When I awoke there was a familiar smell of fresh bacon and sweet pancakes filling the house. I ran into the kitchen and Lindsey was there preparing breakfast. I kind of chuckled because everything was just too good to be true. I was in this amazing house getting everything I ever wanted. She asked me what I would like to do that day. I shrugged my shoulders and she suggested that we go to Toys-R-Us later. I excitedly accepted the offer and chowed down on my bacon and pancakes. After breakfast I went up to my room and started to explore. Yesterday, I noticed all of the toys and things they had available to play with but between dinner and my bedtime story I didn't get a chance to check them out. I played with the toys for most of the morning, building Lego houses and playing make-believe with Hot Wheel cars. I felt happy. I felt like a kid.

As I was playing, my thoughts drifted back to my family. I missed them so much but I never felt this feeling with my mom when I was at home. I actually don't remember my mom ever reading me a book or tucking me into bed. She was always gone. Or if she was home, there was always a party. My sister Jatia was more of a mother figure than my mom. I used to take showers with her, and she even taught me how to cook. There were things she taught me that weren't good like how to steal. We didn't steal toys or anything like that. We would have to steal food from the grocery store to eat. Sometimes my mom would not come back for weeks and we would run out of food she left for us. So, Jatia taught us how to steal and not get caught. One time for Alex's birthday we stole a birthday cake and birthday decorations just so we could throw him a little party. That was my normal. I never knew that parents really treated kids like Lindsey had been treating me. I never wanted to leave.

13

Toys, Truth and a Tall Story

Later that day, as promised, Lindsey said that we were leaving to go shopping. She said she had to pick up some food for Thanksgiving and that we would stop at the toy store afterwards. As we left the house, it started snowing. If you have ever been to the midwest you know how beautiful it is seeing the white snow fall onto the bright orange and red leaves. I usually hate fall because that means Thanksgiving and Christmas was right around the corner. And I don't have good memories of those holidays with my mom. Yet, I felt excited for the first time riding along with Lindsey. We went to a couple of different grocery stores. After we got everything we needed, we headed to Toys-R-Us. On the way there it started to sleet. Lindsey fumbled with the controls on the Range Rover before pulling over. She said that the truck was new and that she forgot how to turn on the defrost. I chuckled to myself because it seemed silly to own a car you didn't know how to work.

I suggested that I look it up in the owner's manual. Although Lindsey didn't know, I had gone through her glove compartment while she ran into a store earlier that day. She smiled telling me I was so bright. We worked together and got the windows defogged. Lindsey thanked me for my help, and we continued our journey. I felt so proud of myself again. To me, it seemed that Gary and Lindsey were perfect parents. Any kid would be so lucky to have them. But like everything in my life, this was temporary. They were not my parents and I knew that after the holiday I would be back with Ms. Jones. Overall, Ms. Jones was a pretty good foster parent. She really kept to herself and worked all the time. But she wasn't anything like Lindsey and Gary. They seemed to really want to be parents and did little things to make you feel special. This was what I wanted. This was the perfect family with the perfect car and a perfect house with a white picket fence. But I faced my reality and knew this was only temporary and that I should enjoy it while it lasted.

Lindsey parked in front of Toys-r-us and I excitedly jumped out of the SUV. I was about to run into the store, but she called my name softly and asked me to grab her hand. I usually wouldn't have listened, but I wanted to impress her and show her that I was a good kid in hopes that they might somehow keep me. When we entered the store she told me that I could pick out one toy that I wanted. She told me to take my time. We had a set of Lincoln Logs at school and I really wanted my own set. I went and found a pretty big set of the wooden toys. As I was walking back to the front of the store, I saw a Hot Wheel truck that I thought would go great with my Lincoln Log set. I grabbed the hot wheel car and I put it in my coat pocket. I found Lindsey talking to a cashier and I got nervous thinking that they might have caught me stealing in the camera. But when I went up to her she smiled and asked me if I found what I was looking for. The apple in my throat slowly disappeared when I smiled back and let her know that I was ready and was happy with my toy. She paid for the Lincoln Logs and we made our way back to the car. When we were halfway home I don't know if it was the guilt that was killing me or just plain stupidity, but I pulled out the Hot Wheel car and showed her and asked if her she liked it. At first, she said that it was pretty cool but after seeing that it was still in the packaging she asked me where I got it. The guilt that was in my throat earlier made its way right back. I thought about lying but I told myself to tell the truth. One of the things that my mom had always told us when we lived with her was the truth will set you free. I never understood that because even when we told the truth we still got beat. To me, I thought the truth will definitely get you beat. However, a lie might work. But I didn't lie this time. I told her that I really wanted both the Lincoln Logs and the Hot Wheel car, but she told me I could only choose one toy. Lindsey pulled the SUV over and parked. She asked me why I thought I needed to steal. I shrugged my shoulders really not knowing why I had done it besides knowing that I wanted it. That is how I survived up to this point in my life, but I did not tell her that,. I just started to cry and told her I was sorry. She wiped my tears and told me that its okay and that humans make mistakes and that is not what matters. She told me what matters is how we make it right and asked me how I should make it right. I asked if she could drive me back to the I store so I could tell them what I did and return the toy. I told her that she should return my Lincoln Logs set because I no longer deserved a gift. Lindsey made a U-turn and we made our way back to the Toy Store. When we got inside Lindsey told me to wait at the customer service desk while she spoke to the manager. A few moments later, a chubby white man with his shirt tucked in came up to me and said, " I hear you have something to tell me?" Wiping tears away, I told him that I stole the toy and handed it to him. He took it out of my hand and I asked him if her was going to call the police on me. He laughed and said no. He did let me know that stealing was against the law and that not many people would be as nice as he was. I told him that I would never steal again and turned to find Lindsey. I couldn't see her at first but I found her at a register buying a huge Hot Wheel racing track set. I asked her why she was buying it and she let me know that it was for me! I was totally shocked. Why would she buy me more toys after I had just stolen from the store? I looked at her strangely and thanked her. You could tell that she knew I was unsure about the gift and she reassured me that it was not a trick. She said it takes a good person to admit what they had done wrong and to make amends for it. She said I had done exactly that. This was so different from any other punishment I had ever received. I got back into the SUV excited to get home to play with my new toys.

As soon as we got back to the house I ran to my room and began to play. I thought to myself, "man this is the life." I remembered the last time I had gotten a toy and it was last year around Valentine's Day. After my mom left my dad because he was involved in dangerous gangs, we never really celebrated Christmas on Christmas Day. My mom would wait until she got her taxes back and tax checks around February or March because that was when she had extra money to buy us Christmas gifts. My mom didn't have a real job but would get tax money for having children. I remember that we went to Toys-R-Us on Valentine's Day because as I was playing with the new wrestling toy my mom had gotten me. Deon, my mom's abusive boyfriend, came home and saw that we had new toys and started screaming at my mom. He was angry because she spent money on us instead of buying more drugs to sell. I remember my mom following Deon up the stairs. He turned around and kicked her down the flight of stairs as she made it to the top. He kicked her so hard that I thought I heard her ribs crack as she flew down the stairs. My mom landed at the bottom of the landing and began to moan and cradle her chest. Deon just walked down the stairs telling her that she knew better. He walked over her and grabbed his coat and left. I rushed over to my mom and she asked me to get her a rag and some ice. Later that day Deon returned with chocolates and flowers and wished my mom a happy Valentine's Day. I will never forget that day, ever in my life.

I pushed the memory to the back of my mind and continued to play with my new toys Lindsey had gotten me.

I guess I lost track of time. There was a knock on my bedroom door and it was Gary. He was home from work and that meant it was time for dinner. He came into my room and asked me how I liked my toys. As I was showing him what I had gotten, he sat on the bed and patted his lap indicating that he wanted me to sit on lap. I got up and crawled up on his lap. He looked down at me and asked me why I stole earlier today. I shrugged as I did earlier and told him I didn't know. I let him know that I had done the right thing and returned the toy car and apologized. Gary said that Lindsey had already told me and that he was proud of me. He told me that while I was staying with them I would not have to steal anything and if I wanted something to ask for it. And they would let me know if I could have it or not. He then went on to say that as long as I followed their rules and did what they said whatever I wanted I would usually get. As he was talking to me, I noticed a lump growing while he talked and it was pressing against my bottom as I sat on his lap. He noticed that I saw his erection. He smiled, winked and put me down as he got up to leave. He told me that dinner would be ready soon and that I should pick up my toys and wash my hands.

I had been touched by Deon and other guys when I lived with my mom but they always forced me to do stuff. So, I really didn't pay Gary's erection any mind. Besides, he and Lindsey were so nice. And I really wanted to show them that I was a good foster kid in hopes that I might be able to stay with them. I wasn't going to do anything that might make them mad at me. When I went down for dinner, Gary and Lindsey were already sitting at the dinner table. Lindsey said we were having tacos, which is something simple, because we were going to eat too much tomorrow on Thanksgiving. She told me that they were hosting their entire family for dinner and that I would get to meet everyone. The rest of the dinner went pretty normal with Gary letting us know how his day at work went. He told me that since he had tomorrow off work that he would read me my bedtime story and tuck me in tonight instead of Lindsey.

After dinner I helped clear the table and went to take a bath. I never liked taking showers. I felt like it is too loud with all the water splashing and that someone could possibly sneak up on me and I wouldn't hear them. As I was getting out of the bathroom I noticed that there were no towels on the towel rack and none in the bathroom closet. I was dripping wet with no way to dry off. I was just about to put on my pajamas while wet but Gary knocked on the door and poked his head in. He asked me if everything was going alright. I told him there weren't any towels. He told me to wait one second, then returned to the bathroom coming in this time. I stood there still dripping wet and now shivering. Gary took the towel he brought in and started to dry me off. He dried my hair first then made his way down my body. As he got to my butt, he took the towel and whipped out my booty crack and made his way to my penis. I had never had anyone besides my sister when I was younger dry me off but at that moment I didn't mind. He didn't do anything creepy, I told myself, maybe he's just a really cool dad. Gary finished drying me and told me to get dressed, brush my teeth, and get ready for bed.

14

Punked by a Punk

I woke up to the smell of Thanksgiving. I went into the kitchen and Lindsey was hard at work making turkey and pies and everything you could imagine eating for Thanksgiving. She had Christmas music playing and already had breakfast ready. We had Belgian waffles. And after we ate, Lindsey told me to go play in my room for a while then get dressed because we had guests coming over for an early dinner. She didn't have to tell me twice. I went straight up to my room and I played with my new Lincoln Logs and Hot Wheel sets. While I was playing with my new toys, I thought to myself that I could live here forever. I had never experienced being treated so well by adults.

Growing up with my mom, I remember only having one Thanksgiving with all the fixings, but it never happened again after that one time. My mind started to wonder and think about my mom and siblings. What were they doing today for Thanksgiving? Were they having as much fun as I was having? I didn't know. But I knew that I'd rather be here than at home with my mom.

After playing for a few hours I put on my nicest outfit, which was just some dark wash jeans and a black turtleneck, and I went downstairs. Gary was watching football and drinking a beer in the TV room and Lindsey was hard at work in the kitchen. I asked her if she needed any help. She said no, but let me lick the spoon from a cake she was making. Soon thereafter, people started arriving at the house. Most were old white people with white hair and others where young like Gary and Lindsey. Everyone seemed super interested in me and why I was there. I heard Lindsey explain that they were doing respite foster care and I was staying with them for a week or so. It really looked like that scene from the movie, *Home Alone,* when everyone in his family came over dressed in ugly sweaters and gathered in the kitchen.

During dinner I didn't say much but I did enjoy all of the delicious food. As I was stuffing my face, I'd listen to them tell stories of the past and share laughter. I wanted that so bad. I wanted a nice family to have warm memories to reminisce with. I finished my dinner and asked Lindsey if I could go back to my room to play. She told me of course, but make sure I don't fall asleep and miss dessert.

I left the table and most of the adults were either still sitting down or had gone to watch the football game on TV. I put my plate into the sink and went upstairs to my room. I had been building little houses and buildings with the Lincoln Logs and used the Hot Wheel cars to make a little city. I was playing pretend when I heard the bedroom door shut behind me. I turned around, and it was Gary. He motioned me to "shh" with his fingers to his mouth and sat on the bed. He patted the bed next to him. I went up to him like I did before and he asked me if I liked Thanksgiving at his house. I told him I loved it and he then asked me if I liked staying there with him and Lindsey. I shook my head yes. At this point he stood up and told me that I will be going back to Ms. Jones house tomorrow but if I did a favor for him I could stay. He would talk to Miss Jennifer and see if they could adopt me! I looked up to him and got very excited and asked him what he needed me to do. He walked to the door, locked it, and came back towards the bed unbuckling his belt. He told me that if I could keep our secret that he would adopt me. He asked me to suck on his penis and I did. it started to grow after a while and I almost threw up. After I gagged a couple more times, he pulled his penis out and he ejaculated into his white Fruit of the Loom underwear. I just stood there looking. I didn't know what to do. Lindsey called up the stairs for me to come down and get dessert. Gary pulled up his pants and grabbed his underwear and put them in the laundry basket after wiping off his penis and told me to get dressed. Although I felt numb, I hurriedly threw my clothes. And for some reason, I felt like I had accomplished something. He told me that if I could keep our secret that I could live here forever. I didn't know how to feel but their family was nice. And I did want to live here. So, I told him that I would keep our secret and he patted my head, opened the door and left the room.

I was so confused. I was so numb. Part of me felt like I made a deal with the devil and on the other hand I would get a home. I also didn't know how to feel about what he made me do. In Ms. Jones' church, the preacher said that man should not be with man and it was an abomination. I had already been baptized in her church a couple times, so I knew I was saved. But what about now? Am I now an abomination? As I was trying to figure out these questions, I had thoughts swirling around in my head. Lindsey called for me from the stairs again and it brought me out of my thoughts. The rest of the night was a blur. I vaguely remember eating a piece of apple pie with vanilla ice cream and trying to watch something on TV. Gary kept looking at me and smiling and he acted like nothing had happened. I felt awkward so I asked Lindsey if I could go to bed. She came upstairs with me and tucked me in. She read me a story then cracked the door leaving the room.

As I fell asleep, I thought about what had happened and what it meant about me. Was I gay? I knew that I had a crush on Cody, my neighbor next door from Mrs. Jones, but I had never thought about doing anything that

Gary just did to me. I don't know what I like. And I'm afraid that I might be gay because of everything that has happened to me. But who cares? I am finally going to have a family. Gary wouldn't lie. I told myself that tomorrow would be the best day of my life.

I was awoken by a gentle nudge. It was Lindsey. She had brought up some oatmeal and toast with orange juice for breakfast. While I was eating, Lindsey started to pack up my clothes and toys. With my mouth full of toast, I asked her what she was doing. She told me that she was packing my stuff because I was going back to Ms. Jones today. I jumped out of bed grabbing her hand crying and asking why they decided not to adopt me. I was crying so hard, one of those gut cries that makes you lose your breath. Lindsey looked confused and pulled her hand back. Tears started to well in her eyes and she asked me why I thought they were going to adopt me. I told her that Gary told me that they would adopt me because I was such a good kid. I knew that was a lie. I knew what I had promised to keep a secret in hopes of being adopted by them. Lindsey lost her temper for the first time since I had been there and she yelled, "Why the fuck would he tell you that?" She stormed out of my room and I followed her plate in hand from my breakfast. I was putting my plate into the sink, and Lindsey was on the phone yelling and asking Gary why he would tell me that. She saw me listening and she went upstairs to her room. I went to my room and started to finish packing. I was hoping that Gary was talking to her and letting her know that he wanted to adopt me like he had promised. I don't know why she got so upset about it though.

A few moments later, Lindsey came back dressed in light-washed blue jeans and a chunky tan sweater. Her blond hair was thrown up in a messy bun and her blue eyes were bloodshot from crying. I had already thrown on some jeans and an old navy sweater. I was sitting on the bed when she walked into the room. She came and sat next to me and asked me why I would make up such a horrible lie? She said that Gary told her that he had never said anything like that to me. He also told her that he noticed that I had a habit of stealing and now lying and that they would not host me again. And Gary said that they would be telling Jennifer about what I had done. While she was talking, I got so lightheaded, the room started spinning. The familiar knot was once again at the back of my throat. I was trying to keep my breakfast down and focus on what Lindsey was saying to me. When my world stopped spinning and my ears stopped ringing, I heard her say that she was disappointed in me and told me to grab my bags.

I grabbed my bag and followed Lindsey out of the room. I didn't even get to say goodbye to Gus. He was behind the doggy gate in the living room. Unlike the last time I rode with Lindsey and sat in the front seat, this time she made me sit in the back seat on the passenger side. I don't know everything Gary had told her but whatever he said she now hated me. She pulled the Range Rover out of the garage and we drove away. I looked behind me and saw their beautiful house with its white picket fence and perfect green grass with a light dusting of snow. It was perfect, but it was full of lies. I might be young, but I grew up in the hood. Once I heard her say that Gary said I lied, I knew I had been punked. As she was driving down the road Lindsey looked at me from the rearview mirror and asked me why would I make up such a lie about Gary telling me that they would adopt me. I wanted to tell her what he had promised me and what I had to do but I knew that she wouldn't believe me. She doesn't even believe my story now, how could I possibly convince her that her husband had molested me? I shrugged and continued my gaze out of the back window. I felt stupid and betrayed, but most of all I felt embarrassed. She continued to talk but to me it sounded like the adults from Charlie Brown. Soon we were on the highway and Lindsey noticed that I wasn't paying her any attention and she stopped talking and turned on the radio.

Now that my dreams of a perfect family with Gary and Lindsey was shattered, I turned my attention to going back to school and hanging out with Cody. After what seemed like an eternity, we pulled up to Catholic Social Services in Muskegon. Lindsey parked along the street and we walked up to the building. The CSS building was grey and almost windowless. It favored a prison. We entered the lobby and I went and took a seat in the corner where I usually sat. Lindsey went up to the reception window and checked in. She told Ms. Penny, the receptionist, that she was in a hurry to get back home and that she could not wait here with me. Ms. Penny told her that she would keep an eye out for me. Lindsey came up to me, patted my head, told me to be a good boy and to stop telling lies because they can hurt people. Then, she was gone.

15

Return to the Woods

I sat in the reception area after Lindsey left and Ms. Penny came from behind the counter to keep me company. I had come to like Ms. Penny over the last year of being in foster care. She was a small little, old white lady with the cutest pixie cut. She had square glasses that framed her warm face perfectly. She was usually the one that stayed with us while we waited for our mom during visits in the visiting room. She was always nice to me and gave me candy. Ms. Penny told me that Miss Jennifer had to finish a meeting and would be right down to take me back to Ms. Jones house. Ms. Penny asked me if I heard the good news yet? I told her I haven't heard yet. She told me that my mom had been approved for a visit next week and that she confirmed the visit. Ms. Penny said that they usually don't alert us kids because they don't want to get our hopes up, but I looked like I needed some good news. She told me that my mom had just called and she was excited to see my siblings and I.

I had not seen my siblings in months. And the last time I saw Jatia, she betrayed me and let me get beat up at the Beasley's. But even still, I missed my family and I was ready to see my mom again. After a while, Miss

Jennifer came from the back and told me to grab my bags. She looked like her usual self, tired of trying to look happy. She asked me how I liked my holiday with Gary and Lindsey. I quickly switched the subject and asked her about the upcoming visit with my mom. Miss Jennifer said that my mom had signed up for some parenting classes and that hopefully she was going to move into her own place and start the process of getting us back. I had given up on the idea of going home. The past year has been so hard. I have lost everything that I knew which was my normal. Did I even want to go home? I wasn't sure. Yes, these last few homes in foster care and my stay at Pine Rest Mental Hospital, I was just trying to live day to day. But I have to say, I did get to eat every day in foster care and I finally had a normal school life. I was torn on how I should feel.

We made our way down the highway in Miss Jennifer's Pontiac towards Whitehall. I wondered how Ms. Jones' Thanksgiving had been with her family. We turned off the highway and made our way down the country roads. It was only the afternoon but it was already dark because it was fall in Michigan. A lot of houses already had their Christmas lights hung and they shimmered against the snow crystals on the ground. It was magical to see. Miss Jennifer pulled into the driveway and the little country cottage sat there. Ms. Jones hadn't put up lights or anything for Christmas. I grabbed my bags and went up to the door. Standing there something made me feel at peace. Even though I didn't love living here I didn't hate it either. This has been one of the only homes that I haven't been harmed. I guess Ms. Jones was alright. I opened the door and found Ms. Jones cooking in the small kitchen. Miss Jennifer followed me in and spoke to Ms. Jones. I went to my room and started to put my stuff away. I pulled out the Hot Wheel track and the Lincoln Logs and I shrugged my shoulders. I told myself that I would never get punked again. Miss Jennifer poked her head in my door and told me that she was going to leave. She asked me if I could walk her to the door so, I did. I watched her get into her Pontiac and back down the driveway.

Ms. Jones was still in the kitchen cooking dinner. She gave me a hug and asked me how my Thanksgiving went. I told her it was okay, but I was glad to be back. We had dinner in the small little kitchen and we watched TV for the rest of the night.

I fell back into my routine of school, Cody's house and chores. Since Cody and I had become best friends we did almost everything together. Winter break was coming, and Cody and his family were going on vacation. He asked me if I wanted to sleepover on the first night of winter break before they left. I told him that I would love that. A couple days later was winter break, and we had a couple weeks off school for Christmas. That day after getting off the bus, I ran home dropped my backpack off and changed my clothes and packed a little overnight bag. I was out of the house in less than five minutes, and I running down the street to Cody's house. When I got there their house was so different then Mrs. Jones. They had lights everywhere! Even their horse stable was decorated for Christmas. I thought to myself that Cody was so lucky. I had been hanging out with Cody so much that I knew the code to the house. I let myself in like I had been doing for weeks, and Cody was busy playing video games in the game room. We played *Mario* for a little while then his mom told us to get our coats on. She let us know that we were going out to eat for dinner. Cody's dad wasn't around much but he was a big jolly guy with a blond combover that was blond but graying. Today was the first time that I had seen him in normal clothes and not in a suit. We made our way to their three-car garage where they had some of the nicest cars I had ever seen in real life. Usually Cody's mom would drive us to baseball practice in a Cadillac SUV but I had never seen his dad's car. His dad a two door black Porsche roadster, and a four-door Cadillac. He pulled out the four-door car and we all hopped in. The inside of the car was way nicer than the outside. It was all leather and the seats in the back were even heated. We drove to little downtown Whitehall, which wasn't more than a couple of shops, restaurants and a small city hall.

Whitehall, Michigan represented its name well. It was all white, except for me and Ms. Jones.

Cody's dad parked in front of a seafood restaurant and looked back at me in the rearview mirror. He asked me if I liked seafood. I told him, "I really didn't like seafood but when I see food, I eat it." Cody rolled his eyes. He hated when I did silly puns, but his parents loved it. We had an amazing dinner. It was my first-time having lobster. It will always be a memory I cherish. I had never experienced anything like it before. We all had to wear gloves and bibs and they gave us this little shell-cracking utensils. Cody and his parents didn't seem phased, but I was too excited. This was the fanciest restaurant I had ever been in. During dinner, in-between cracking lobster shells, we talked about school and how Cody and I were doing in baseball. Cody was a great athlete, but I was not so good. I rarely ever hit the ball when it was my turn to bat. But when I did make it to a base, I was fast and good at stealing bases. Cody's parents asked me what I had planned for the winter break. I shared with them the good news about my upcoming visit with my mom. I never really talked about my birth family or being in foster care with Cody or his family. I guess I wanted to keep that part of my life separate so I could feel a little more normal. They could sense that I didn't want to talk much about my family or the holidays and quickly changed the subject. They started talking about their upcoming vacation and how excited they were to go skiing. Cody told me that I was welcome to ride his motorbike and go-cart while they were gone if I promised to be careful. I shook my head indicating that I heard him. Cody's mom tried to include me in the conversation again and asked me if I knew how to ski. I told her no and acted like I was preoccupied with cracking the shells and eating.

As they were talking about what they were going to do on vacation, I thought about the time with my mom when we were living in a nicer neighborhood. My siblings and I were friends with the kids who lived across the street. One summer they told us that their parents were taking them to

Disney for a week. We didn't pay it any mind but the day they left they asked us to feed their cat every day. We agreed to feed the cat and they showed us where their spare key was located. The next day, while we were in their house feeding the cat, Jatia was looking around the house to see what we could steal. We found some jewelry in their parents' room on the dresser and we left. Later that day, our Uncle Feeky came over to the house and saw us with really nice jewelry on. At first, Jatia lied and told him we found it. But of course, my big mouth told him where we had gotten it from. My Uncle asked Jatia to show him the house and how to get it. We went back over to our neighbor's house with Uncle Feeky and one of his friends I didn't know. I stayed outside the house and told them I would be a lookout. The truth was I was just too afraid of getting caught. I thought that they were just going to get the rest of the jewelry, but they came out with a big screen TV and computer.

I followed Uncle Feeky back to my mom's house. He went downstairs to the basement where he had a little room he stayed in every once in a while. He put the TV on the floor and I sat on his bed. Alex, Tim and I all stayed in the house while Jatia, Uncle Feeky and his friend, went back and forth grabbing more and more stuff out of our neighbor's house. I don't know why they didn't think that one of our other neighbors wouldn't call the police when they saw three people hauling stuff out of one house and into the other, but cops came shortly after they had taken almost everything of value. The cops knocked on the door and asked to search the house. My other Uncle Tyrone had just gotten to the house from work, so he didn't know what was going on. So, he let the police search the house because he thought they were full of shit. Uncle Feeky hid behind the washer and dryer in the basement and put as much stuff as he could under his bed and asked us to sit on the bed. When the police came downstairs to the room they found my three siblings and I all sitting down on the bed that clearly had large items under it. We were all sitting there just looking at them. I know we looked suspicious as hell. The police told us to go upstairs with our Uncle Tyrone as they searched the basement. Of course, they found all of the stolen stuff as and they found my Uncle Feeky hiding behind the washer and dryer. My uncle never told them that we helped him steal. He got arrested and ultimately spent years in prison. I didn't see him again until years later when I was an adult. Cody's family talking about vacation brought that memory up.

We finished our lobster dinner and headed back to Cody's house. When we got back to his house his mom brought down some boxes that were wrapped in Christmas paper. I thought she was going to give them to Cody, but she gave them to me! I was so surprised! I hurriedly unwrapped the presents throwing the beautiful wrapping paper everywhere. It was a huge *Indiana Jones* Lego set. I loved Legos and I loved *Indiana Jones*. I sat the set aside and opened my second gift. The second box had a bunch of socks, underwear and clothes in my size. I thanked Cody's parents and gave them a hug. I had never had a friend's parent care so much about me.

Cody and I played Nintendo the rest of the day, late into the night. After we were tired of playing games, we headed up to Cody's room. This was the first time I had stayed this late and I had never spent the night before. I had butterflies in my stomach because Cody was so cool and so nice. Like most of the house, his room was large and really nice. He even had a bathroom. We were brushing our teeth and Cody finished before I did. After he washed his mouth out, he stripped down to his underwear to put on his pajamas. The butterflies almost burst out of my belly when I saw him. Cody was definitely my first crush.

The next morning, I gathered my overnight bag and my presents, and walked back to Ms. Jones house. She had already left for work, so I was by myself for the day. I had so many toys now that were mine! I played the whole day building things with my Lincoln Logs and Legos. Ms. Jones came home at her regular time and made dinner. While we were sitting down eating she let know that she was going into work tomorrow because she had to take me to Catholic Social Services for a family visit. This time I didn't get excited though. I told myself that my mom probably wouldn't show up and I wasn't going to get my hopes up. Ms. Jones went to work, and I stayed home that day. I spent most of the morning cleaning everything on the list that she left. I went over to Cody's and grabbed his go-cart out of his garage and took it for a spin. I spent the rest of the day driving the go-cart and thinking about Cody. I drove it until the gas ran out and I had to push it back to the garage. It was almost dark before I made it back home and the house was still dark. Ms. Jones hadn't made it home yet. It had started snowing so she probably had to stop and put her snow tires on. I waited for her in the living room and rocked on the chair. Ms. Jones came home with a pizza. She sat it on the table and went straight into her room. I grabbed a couple slices myself and went to my room. I wanted to get to sleep early because I didn't want to be tired.

The next morning, I went into the kitchen expecting to see Ms. Jones eating breakfast but she wasn't. She was warming up the truck. I asked her what she was doing, and she told me that she had to go into to work. I reminded her that I had a visit and she told me that she would be back in time to drive me there. She pulled the truck out of the driveway and left. I was so anxious the whole day that I did nothing but watch TV and go to the window and look out at the empty road hoping that she would come home early. She didn't and as the day went by, I got more and more agitated. I knew the visit was supposed to be at 5 p.m. and it took us about an hour to drive to CSS. My agitation turned into full anger when the clock struck 5 p.m. and I thought that I missed my family visit. Ms. Jones came home around 5:30 p.m. and when she came through the door I was so visibly upset. I asked why she was late, and she didn't take it very well. She told me that I was just a foster child and I did not dictate what she did and when she did it. I went and sat down and Ms. Jones went to the phone. I heard her talking and I heard her say Ms. Penny's name. That meant she was calling CSS. She talked for a little bit more and I tried to catch every word she said. She hung up the phone and and came into the living room. She told me that my mom hadn't showed up and that my siblings had been sent home already so there wasn't a point to drive there. I started to scream at the top of my lungs and hyperventilate. I was so upset. I was so exhausted of hoping and waiting to see my mom. And to make it worse, I hadn't seen my siblings and it would have been nice to see them before Christmas. Why didn't Ms. Jones care? Why did she decide to go to work and not take me to CSS. I hadn't thrown a fit like this since before I went to Pine Rest. I guess I snapped mentally. I was eight years old and I was constantly thinking about things that no eight-year-old should ever have to think about.

I stopped screaming and I asked what we were having for dinner. She told me that after the way I just acted that she was not going to make dinner. She told me to make a bowl of cereal. I had been eating cereal all day waiting for this bitch I thought to myself. I started eating the cereal and my anger was replaced with sadness and I started to cry. I was shoving cereal in my mouth and had salty tears running down my cheeks. Mrs. Jones came back into kitchen and told me to stop crying. For some reason that made me cry more. She then said that I was ungrateful and that my mom was a bitch and that she should have to deal with this and not her. I flipped out and slammed my fist on the table. I hit my bowl and cereal and mill flew all over Ms. Jones and the kitchen. She cursed me out and went to her room. She came out with a belt and beat me with it. She just kept swinging. She hit me at least twenty times and the last few times it felt like she was taking out all of her frustrations on me. In between the blows, she demanded that I stop crying. I did. I just sat there and let her hit me. I didn't even try to run.

Ms. Jones threw me into my room and slammed the door. I was so angry and hurt I didn't know which emotion to have at that moment. How could my mom not come? Was Ms. Jones telling the truth? Maybe my mom would have come if I had been there on time. Ultimately, I decided that it was Ms. Jones' fault that my mom hadn't come. Over the next few days, I pouted and complained about everything. I didn't even care that it was Christmas. On Christmas morning, Ms. Jones had two gifts for me on the kitchen table. Even though I was still mad at her about the visit, I was excited to receive presents. There was a big bag and a small box. I opened the small box first. It was a Tasmanian Devil Chia Pet. I love The Looney Toons, so I was pretty excited for the gift. Ms. Jones told me to be careful as I opened the second gift. I looked on the inside of the bag and I saw a small aquarium. What the hell did she get me. I pulled out the little plastic rectangle aquarium and it was a frog! An orange and red fire belly frog to be exact. Mrs. Jones told me that it would be my responsibility to take care of the frog. She told me that I would have to clean the aquarium and change the water once a week.

I named my pet frog Blaze because he reminded me of fire. It was a simple gesture, but I did feel better about not seeing my family. I was so lonely, now I had a friend. I don't think you are supposed to play with a frog like it's a pet dog but the first day I had Blaze out hopping around, I even made little houses for him with my Lincoln Logs. Ms. Jones made a special Christmas dinner. And we watched old Christmas movies throughout the night. I hated this Christmas. It wasn't even about not getting nice presents. It was about not having family to share it with. I was ready to go back to school and to see Cody. The next few days of Christmas break weren't eventful. Ms. Jones went to work, and I tried my best to keep myself entertained. The last night of the break, I got myself ready to go to school the next morning.

16

Black Booger Burger

I couldn't wait to meet Cody on the bus the first day back to school. He was sitting in our normal seat when I got on the bus. Just like that, things went back to how they had been before the holiday break. I spent as much time as I could with Cody after school. And we did all of the same extracurricular stuff like sports and clubs.

Over the next few weeks, spring was approaching and as the sun was staying out longer, I was getting darker staying out in it. One day during recess, one of the girls in my class who had been bullying me all year long about being a foster kid started making fun of me on the playground. She was commenting about how dark my skin was getting and she started calling me "black booger burger." She had been bullying me for a while and I had been ignoring it. But, that day was different. I guess I had a lot of pent-up anger from not being able to visit my family. I ran up to her and told her to shut up. She just laughed and continued to call me names. I grabbed her blond hair at the roots and dragged her to the ground. She started screaming, but there were so many kids screaming and playing that the recess watcher didn't hear her. I believe this was one of the first times that I blacked out in anger. When I realized what I was doing, I was already slamming her head on the metal bars of the jungle gym . There was so much blood and I saw a huge gash in her skull, even the white meat was visible.

I was still hitting her when someone grabbed me from the back, picked me up and carried me back into the school. I had blood all over my hand and clothes. I'm sure I looked crazy. I didn't know what had gotten into me. I was escorted to my teacher's classroom, where she and the principal were waiting for me. The principal told me that the police had been called and that the little girl would need medical attention. He told me that he had also called a social worker, and they were on their way to pick me up. I asked him if I was suspended and he gave me a worried look. He then told me that I was being expelled and would not be welcomed back to the school. I asked if the girl would get into trouble as well. They said no and that she was the victim of a random attack! I tried to tell them what she had been saying to me, but they didn't care. So, I lost it and started having a temper tantrum. I started throwing books and ripping things off of the wall. I didn't think it was fair that the girl wasn't getting in trouble. I asked my teacher if she knew that the girl was picking on me. She shrugged her shoulders like she didn't know when, in fact, I had told her several times over the last few weeks.

The bell rang and kids were waiting outside the classroom to come in. I saw Cody looking in the window and we locked eyes. I could tell he was scared of me. That broke my heart, and I picked up a chair and threw it at my teacher. I felt like it was her fault for taking the girl's side. Now, my crush thinks I'm a crazy person covered in blood. My teacher ducked and dodged getting hit by the chair. Following the chaos, a police officer came into the classroom and handcuffed me and took me to the principal's office. As if I was wasn't embarrassed enough already, nearly all of the school saw me in handcuffs on my walk to the principal's office. The officer waited in the office with me until Miss Jennifer got there. He told her that I was being expelled and was to leave the school grounds. He also said that I was lucky that the little girl's parents did not want to press charges because they knew I was a foster child. They just asked that I be removed from the school.

Miss Jennifer went to my classroom, gathered all of my belongings and came back to the office. She asked the police officer to escort us to her car with me. Once we reached the car, the officer took the handcuffs off, put me into the backseat and closed the door. When Jennifer got into the car, she didn't say anything. I started to panic and asked her if I was going back to Pine Rest Mental Hospital. I couldn't fully contemplate what would happen after I hit that girl. Things were going so well, and I was finally happy. I was so mad at myself as I sat there once again in the back of this Pontiac. It seemed like I could never catch a break, and I was starting to feel exhausted. Miss Jennifer finally spoke and told me that I was very lucky that the girl only needed stitches and that her parents weren't pressing charges. She told me that if they would have pressed charges against me that I would go to a juvenile detention center, which is a lot like jail.

We drove towards Ms. Jones house, and my anxiety started to fade. We pulled into the driveway and Jennifer asked, "Where is Ms. Jones' truck?" I told her that she didn't get home until around five or five-thirty so I usually played at Cody's house until she got home. We sat in the car and waited for Ms. Jones to come home.

While we waited, I thought about what would happen next. I knew Ms. Jones would be really upset, especially after everything I did when my family visit was cancelled. I really wasn't too concerned about her though. I wasn't even sure if she would still want to be my foster parent. I was so used to moving around at this point that it didn't matter. Then, I thought about school, and how upset I was. I was finally in a school that I was doing good in and actually liked. Unlike the schools in Muskegon, Whitehall Elementary had new books and a desk. The basketballs in the gym actually had air in them and smelled like new rubber. I didn't have many friends, but the ones I had, I really liked. And finally there was Cody. What would happen to us? I thought about the way his face looked when he saw me having a breakdown in the classroom. He looked so shocked and sad at the same time. I wondered if he would still be my friend after seeing that. The unknown was something that I hated. So, instead of trying to figure it out, I just assumed the worst case scenario. Cody wasn't going to be my friend ever again. Sadly, I wasn't too far off.

Ms. Jones' red Ford F250 pulled up and Miss Jennifer told me to stay in the car. I thought, "Here we go again." I figured that Miss Jennifer was just getting my things. I tried to listen, but their voices were muffled by the wind. After a few moments I stopped trying to hear what was going on and decided that whatever was going to happen I was going to learn from it. Miss Jennifer came back to the car and opened my door. "Get into the house," she told me. I slowly crept out of the car and followed her orders. I went straight to my room and started packing my things in garbage bags. Ms. Jones called me from the kitchen and I hurriedly stuffed as much stuff as I could while leaving behind Blaze, my pet frog. I went into the kitchen with my bags and Ms. Jones let out a sarcastic laugh. Miss Jennifer kneeled down to my eye level and said, "Ms. Jones has decided to give you one more chance to live here with her. Being that you were expelled today, you won't be able to attend any school in the county." Miss Jennifer said, "I have some contacts at a school for kids with special needs." She explained that I would most likely attend that school. Ms. Jones dismissed me to my room and told me that I was on punishment until further notice.

The next day before she went to work, Ms. Jones woke me up and said that I was not allowed to go to Cody's house under any circumstances. She had left a to do list and asked that I finish it before I do anything else. That day I did just that. I shoveled the snow out of the driveway and stacked wood along the house. I had almost finished stacking it when I saw the school bus coming down the street. I saw Cody get off and my heart skipped a beat. Ms.

Jones told me that I wasn't allowed to go to Cody's house, but she never said anything about talking to him on the road. I ran down the road shouting his name to get his attention. He turned around and stopped. When I got to him, he turned and looked around as if he was looking to see if anyone was watching us. I asked him, "What was the matter? And what were they saying at school?" Cody said, "There was an assembly today and the principal said that you had a nervous breakdown because you suffered so much abuse as a child. He said that we should keep the students involved in the incident in our prayers." Cody also told me that the principal told everyone that I was not allowed on the school campus and that I was expelled. Cody asked me, "Why did you do it?" And I couldn't really give him a real reason besides that she called me a "black booger burger." Shaking his head, he sighed and put his hand on my shoulder. "My mom and dad don't want me hanging out with you anymore. They think you are dangerous. I know you aren't, and that you are full of fun and happiness. But, what you did at the school has everyone talking. And since I was your friend, my parents don't want the kids to pick on me. I like you Karlos. I really do. I'm sorry."

He gave me a long hug and let go. He turned around and started walking towards his house. I stood there literally frozen in place. Tears welled in my eyes as I watched Cody walk away. I couldn't believe he told me that he liked me too. And the way he said it made me know it was in the same way I liked him. But our friendship was over now, and he was the only person I felt close to. The tears that had welled up could no longer hold themselves back and I started to cry. I wasn't sure why I was crying but I knew I was hurt. And to make it worse I wasn't hurt by what Cody said I was hurt by my actions that made him say it. Why did I let her get me so angry?

17

Short Bus & The Quiet Room

The next few days were the same. I would complete the chores list that Ms. Jones left for me. When I was done, I would just sit in the house and wait for the next day. After about a week, Miss Jennifer called Ms. Jones to let her know that I had a spot at a special needs school. She said I could start the following Monday. I didn't know what to expect. I had been in special ed before, but I had never been to a school that was only for special needs children. Nonetheless, I was excited to get out of the house and actually see other people.

The following Monday, Ms. Jones stayed home to help me get onto the bus. I got up, got dressed and had cereal at the kitchen table. I was looking out of the window and I saw a short yellow school bus pull up in front of the house. The bus had a handicap ramp in the middle of it. When I got to the door, I noticed that more than half of the bus were filled with motorized wheelchairs. The kids strapped in the wheelchairs were clearly mentally challenged. I got onto the bus and made my way down the aisle. I sat down towards the back where there was a couple of regular bus seats.

I will always remember the smell of that bus. The scent was a mixture of stale urine and cotton candy. I sat down in my seat and tried not to make eye contact with anyone. I stared at my feet not wanting to look up. I snuck a glance at the kid sitting in the wheelchair closest to my seat. He was drooling and making a strange sound that was being drowned out by the sound of country music playing on the bus speakers. The bus stopped a couple more times, lowering the handicap ramp and the driver assisted locking the wheelchairs into place. After the last pick up, the bus got onto the highway for what felt like an hour. During that time, I thought about Cody and how much I loved riding the bus with him and how different this bus was.

The bus pulled off the highway and made its way towards a large brown brick building with high windows. This school looked a lot like the Pine Rest building and my stomach dropped. The bus ramp lowered and the driver helped the kids in wheelchairs out of the bus. I was the last student off. A lady with long brown hair down her back with bangs in the front was waiting for me. She looked really sweet and welcomed me with a warm handshake. She said, "I'm Miss Tammy, your teacher's assistant. And I will pick you up and drop you off to the bus every day". Tammy took my hand and guided me through the school. The hallways were stark white with white linoleum floors. Bright fluorescent lights lined the ceiling. This place did not look like any school I had ever been to! Tammy showed me around the school and we stopped at a door that was close to the principal's office. She opened the door and I looked inside. It was a small padded room. The room was lined with floor-to-ceiling, blue padding, you know, like the ones used in gym class. There was nothing else in the room but one single fluorescent light and a small rectangular window in the door. I asked Miss Tammy, "What was the room used for?"

"This is our quiet room," she responded. "A place you go when you feel out of control and are a danger to yourself or others."

I looked at her and told her that I would never have to use that room. She smiled and kind of chuckled a little bit and said, "We will see." She showed me the rest of the school including the nurse's station, bathrooms and the playground. When we got to my class, there were kids sitting at large tables, two or three of them at one table. Some kids were in automatic wheelchairs like the ones I saw on the bus. Some kids were drawing while others were staring in a daze. Miss Tammy showed me to my table that was close to her desk, and then went to assist the teacher with another student. They didn't have a desk, instead they had large tables and kids with wheelchairs used as well. Moments later, the teacher came up to my desk and introduced herself. She said her name was Mrs. White and that she would be my teacher while I was attending this school. At first meeting, Mrs. White didn't seem so bad. She was in her mid-thirties with a bright smile and golden hair. She had on a red turtleneck sweater and blue jeans with eyes that matched. She seemed like a cool teacher. I thought to myself, this won't be as bad as I thought.

Then, I was given a packet to work on. It was filled with very easy work. Although it was really hard to pay attention to my work with all of the sounds that my classmates were making. Around 11 o'clock, Miss Tammy got up from her desk and announced that it was time for recess. Mrs. White went to help the students in wheelchairs while the able-bodied kids went with Miss Tammy. The playground was a huge wooden castle with little passageways that ran from one side to another, making it easy to play tag. So far, this school wasn't that bad. I was running through the wooden castle and really enjoying my time when my mind turned to Cody. The knot in my throat came back, and tears started to well up in my eyes. I missed him and his family. I began to get angry but I calmed myself down, not wanting to get into trouble at this new school.

Recess ended and we all returned to class. Mrs. White turned on Cartoon Network on the TV that was mounted in the corner of the room. The *Scooby-Do Show* was playing. Shortly after, someone brought in a big metal lunch cart, like the ones you see in hospitals. That day we had pizza and green beans with chocolate milk. We watched cartoons and worked on our packets until Miss Tammy brought us back to the bus at the end of the day. This was so different from Whitehall Elementary.

The first couple of weeks were great. Nothing really happened besides a few students freaked out during class and were put into straitjackets and the soft room. I managed to fly under the radar and not cause too much trouble until Cody saw me get off the bus one day after school. He was with his baseball team and they all started laughing, taunting me for riding a "short bus." I thought Cody would defend me. Instead, he joined in with the jokes and laughter against me. I started screaming back at them and picked up a couple rocks and threw them down the road. One of them connected with one of the boys and cut his head open. I turned and ran home.

Since my new school was in another town, Mrs. Jones got home before me. She was in the kitchen cooking dinner when I ran into the house out of breath. She asked, "Why are you outta breath boy?" Of course, I lied and said, "I just wanted to get home to play with my toys." She shrugged and turned her attention back to making dinner.

I was in my room laying on my bed thinking about what happened at the bus stop. How could Cody join in with them making fun of me? I loved him. I thought he was my best friend. I thought about his friend who I hit in the head with the rock. I wondered what they would say. I didn't have to wonder for too long because there was a knock on the front door. I heard Ms. Jones answer the door and welcome someone in. She called for me and I got off my bed and went into the kitchen. When I walked in, I saw

Cody's mom and another white lady I did not know, but they both looked very upset. Ms. Jones asked me what happened at the bus stop. I shrugged mumbling "nothing" while keeping my head down and looking at my feet. The one lady I didn't know yelled that I was a dangerous monster and that I almost killed her son. Cody's mom who seemed to have calmed down seeing me so ashamed told her to calm down and not be so dramatic. She told Ms. Jones that I threw a rock at the lady's son and now he needed stitches. Ms. Jones asked me, "Is that true?" I didn't answer. She told me to apologize and I didn't answer. I just stood there defeated and angry. The lady told Ms. Jones that I was lucky that Cody's mom convinced her not to call the police on me and press charges because I was a foster child and had already been through a lot lately. She told Ms. Jones to keep me on a leash or else. And they stormed out of the house.

I turned and ran to my room slamming the door. Ms. Jones didn't come and yell at me like she usually did. Instead, I heard her finish dinner and turned on the television. I heard the intro for the *Touched by and Angel* show, and I tried to imagine what the episode was about. I didn't eat that night. I fell asleep while tears dripped from the tip of my nose onto the pillow. I dreaded getting up the next morning. I did not want to get back on the short bus. I was so ashamed. I woke up with a chip on my shoulder and I knew it wasn't going to be a good day. I got dressed and went to wait for the bus. As I was standing outside, my old bus from Whitehall Elementary went past me with all of the kids I now hated. The short bus pulled up shortly after and I got on. I don't think I will ever get used to the smell or the sounds that were made by the kids on this bus. I started to appreciate the country music the bus driver played because it helped drown out some of the noise. Everything was annoying to me. The drool dripped from one kid's mouth and slid down their wheelchair.

The bus pulled up to the school and Miss Tammy was waiting there in her usual spot. She reached out to take my hand like we had been doing, but this time I withdrew my hand with an attitude. She didn't seem to mind and let me walk to the building by myself. The beginning of the day was normal until we went to recess. I didn't want to go outside for recess and Mrs. White told me that I had to. I told her that I'm not going outside and that the "retards" didn't have go so why did I have to? Mrs. White told me what I said was inappropriate and that I would have to go to the quiet room for a time out. She approached me and I started freaking out. I started punching and kicking. Miss Tammy came over to help hold me down while Mrs. White called the office for backup. Three office nurses came into our class and helped my teachers get me into a straitjacket and put a mesh screen over my face.

They strapped me into a wheelchair and rolled me down the hall to the soft room. They opened the door and sat me in the middle of the room, laying me on my back. They closed the door and it went quiet. I started screaming and I continued to scream at the top of my lungs. I stayed in the quiet room for the rest of the day. The nurses came with Miss Tammy when it was time to take me to the bus. I was so tired of being isolated that I didn't put up a fight. I had so much built up anger inside like a teapot of hot water. I was about to boil over by the time I got home.

Ms. Jones was cooking when I walked into the door. She told me to take a seat at the table. She asked, "What happened at school today?" I rolled my eyes and didn't answer. She then slapped me across my face so hard my ears rang. I had had enough! I flipped the kitchen table and started throwing anything I could get my hands on. I blacked out in rage. When I came to the kitchen was destroyed and Mrs. Jones was in her room with the door closed. I could hear her talking on the phone saying, "Come get this nigga out of my fucking house," I went back to my room and began packing. I didn't even care anymore. I was so desensitized of feeling anything anymore.

I had finished packing when Ms. Jones came to my room. She told me that Miss Jennifer couldn't get here until tomorrow. She said that my black ass would be out of her house bright and early. I said "great," and she just started beating me. She started punching me in my chest and I didn't fight back this time. I just crawled into a ball and took the hits. At least I could feel the pain of getting hit because I couldn't feel any other emotion. She finally tired herself out and left me there on the floor in a ball not making a sound. I climbed into bed for the last time in this house. I had been through so much here but I wasn't sad to leave. I also hoped that moving foster homes meant that I could go to a different school. I was so tired of getting on that short bus and I couldn't stand the smell of soiled diapers and spit. I hadn't seen my siblings in months. And I was so hurt by Cody not liking me anymore. He was my first love and my first heartbreak.

18

Too many Homes to Count

Early the next morning Miss Jennifer came and I was ready, sitting on the bed with my bags packed. She came to the room and helped me grab my bags. I walked down the short hallway past the small kitchen where Ms. Jones was sitting at the table with her arms crossed and a frown on her face. I walked out of the small cottage and got into the Pontiac Trans Am and never looked back. I never saw anyone from Whitehall again.

Usually I would be bombarding Jennifer with questions, "Where am I going?" "How long will I be there?" But, to be completely honest, I didn't care. Anywhere but that isolated place would be better. As we drove back towards Muskegon the scenery changed from woods to buildings. Once we were downtown Miss Jennifer started making familiar turns. Before we pulled up to the building that I knew I was Child Haven, I started crying. Miss Jennifer turned and kinda laughed when she asked me jokingly, "It isn't that bad in there is it?" Before I could answer, she told me that she was just there to pick up some paperwork and that I was going to a foster home with a lot of kids my age. I started to get excited, but I reminded myself that there hasn't been a good foster home yet, so why would this one be any different?

Miss Jennifer came back to the car with a stack of papers, and we made our way to the next foster home. We pulled up to a huge brick, two-story home with a wraparound wooden porch. This area was downtown Muskegon, so this house was nice but you could tell that it was well-worn. Before we could get out of the car, there were at least five kids that came pouring out of the house and watched us from the porch. Miss Jennifer said hello to the kids and helped me bring my bags into the house. There was a loud woman's voice telling the kids to come inside and go to their rooms. And then, I heard shuffling coming towards the front door. When the voice arrived at the door, it was a huge black woman with bright red lipstick and a stringy wig that badly needed to be brushed. She welcomed us to the house. Miss Jennifer introduced me and said she had to get going. Miss Jennifer bent down and told me to behave and to try to make the best out of this. I shook my head yes. I watched her leave the house, jump into her Pontiac and drive away. I stood there with my bags looking at this woman - not even knowing her name. The kids had heard Miss Jennifer close the door and were peeking down the stairs. The lady told me to grab my bag and to "come on." The kids scattered to different rooms as I followed her up the stairs. We made our way to a long hallway. At the end of it, there was a door to another set of stairs. She said that she couldn't fit up the spiral stairs but told me to go up them and there would be two beds. The one with fresh sheets folded on it would be my bed. I started up the stairs and I turned to ask her, "What is your name?" She simply said, "Big Momma" and shut the door.

I went up the stairs and found a small room with angled ceilings. It was literally an attic with two twin beds with flimsy mattresses and a dresser in the corner. I found the bed Big Momma was speaking of but wished she would have made the bed. It was super stained with urine and I would have rather not seen what I had to sleep on. I put my bags down and searched for a bath towel. I found some in the closet. I used one to cover the top of the mattress before I put the sheets on. It made me feel a little better that there was some sort of a barrier. Looking back at it now, that towel didn't protect me from the bed bugs that infested the house. I finished making the bed and just sat on it. I was still sore from the beating last night. I hadn't slept very well, not knowing where I would end up today.

I guess I slept most of the day because when I woke up it smelled like it was dinnertime. I went downstairs in a haze not knowing if I was still sleeping or not. I found my way to the kitchen by following the delicious smell, which grew stronger as I got nearer. There was so much food on the dining table - fried chicken, corn bread, and potato salad. It looked like a perfect Thanksgiving dinner in the middle of spring. As I was taking it all in, I heard a stampede of footsteps. Before I could grab a plate and get some of the food, the dozen other foster kids circled the table like vultures, and hands just started grabbing everything. I froze with anxiety and stole a look at Big Momma. She just looked satisfied with herself, folding her arms and smirking. Kids started fighting over food, pushing and shoving each other, while others found a place to eat either at the table or on the living room couch. They all acted like what was going on was normal. I was slowing recovering from my panic attack and was able to grab two drumsticks and the last spoonful of the potato salad. The table was trashed, and Big Momma had disappeared. I took my plate to the attic room and sat on the bed. "What the hell was I doing here?" I asked myself. I thought I would be happy leaving Ms. Jones' house and have more kids around, but this was not what I had in mind. Setting my plate on the nightstand next to bed, I laid my head down on the pillow trying not to think about what the mattress looked like underneath. I stared at the ceiling until I fell asleep.

I woke up to screams and laughing that was coming from downstairs. I sat up on the bed and just cried. I felt so isolated, so alone. I felt like I kept losing everyone I was close to. I missed Cody. And I never thought I would say this, but I missed the quietness of the woods in Whitehall. A knock on the door distracted me from my self-pity and I wiped my face. I said "come in" thinking it might be Big Momma. One of the kids came in. I hadn't seen him yesterday at all. He came in saying hello and introducing himself as Jamal. I asked him if he was new here also? He chuckled, smiling showing he had silver caps. "No," he responded. Before I could ask him another question, he told me that he likes to let the new foster kids get the room for the first night because they usually cry. He said he didn't like seeing people cry. I looked down at my feet because I had cried most of the day yesterday and this morning. Jamal told me that breakfast would be soon and that school would start right after breakfast. I had completely forgotten about school. I knew I wasn't going back to the crazy school but where would I be going? I asked Jamal what school he went to. He smiled again, this time more of a smirk, and told me that we all are homeschooled!

Breakfast was no better than dinner last night. The other kids were just as crazy while making their plate. This time I jumped into the mix because I was hungry. I managed to grab a banana and a granola bar. I didn't see Foster Lady. In fact, I hadn't seen her since dinner last night. I brought my food up to my room and Jamal was already there eating. I asked him if he had seen the Foster Lady. He told me she was probably still at the casino. He said that unless there was a new kid being dropped off by their caseworker, the Foster Lady isn't usually at home. The eldest three kids were always in charge and I had to listen to them otherwise I would get into trouble. This wasn't that strange to me. Ms. Jones left me home alone all the time when she was at work and I never had any problems.

I went outside after I ate my breakfast to go sit on the porch. I really just wanted some time to myself and space away from the other kids. I didn't even know what part of Muskegon I was in. When Miss Jennifer was driving me here, I recognized some parts of the neighborhood because it was where the Beasleys lived. I decided to go explore and walk around the neighborhood. I was almost nine years old, too young to be walking alone but the foster lady didn't seem to care what we did. I put my shoes on and hit the streets.

The spring sun was peeking its head above the horizon. I walked down the street until I got to an intersection. There was a white duplex across the street with peeled paint. It was the classic duplex you see in Muskegon, an older house that had been converted. There were two doors on the front porch - one A and the other B. I heard music coming from the upstairs and voices yelling. It sounded like a party. I stepped back into the street to see if I could see into the house. All of a sudden a man came to the window and screamed at me, "What the fuck are you looking at nigga?" The only thing I could mumble from my shocked mouth was a confused question, "Dad?"

19

Daddy Wasn't There

The last time I saw my father, he tricked me into unlocking the front door while my mom was gone. He broke into her room and stole her stash of drugs out of the mini fridge in her room. I will never forget that day because she went out, found him and ran him over with her car. She had dropped us off at our auntie's house and when she came back my dad's skin was literally skinned off his body. My aunt and mom made a makeshift hospital in the basement, bandaged him up and nursed him back to health. The next day, my dad was in so much pain and looked so horrible I started to cry. My mom told me to stop crying and that is what happens when crackheads steal. That was the last time I saw him and that was years ago.

At first, he didn't seem to recognize me, but then he yelled, "Karlos?"

I shook my head yes and he shouted to whoever was in the house, "That's my son downstairs. That's my baby." He left the window and seconds later he was coming out of door A. He ran to the street and picked me up in a big bear hug. He smelled like malt liquor and weed and was clearly intoxicated. He took my hand and brought me into the house. There was a flight of stairs that lead into the apartment upstairs. Inside there were a couple of people smoking and dancing. They seemed to have been there for a while, looking at all the cigarette butts collected in the ashtray.

He introduced me to everyone and asked what I was doing there. Did he even know I was in foster care I wondered? I told him that I was in a foster home across the street. I let him know that I had just been placed there and I asked him where he had been.

"I knew you were in foster care and I am trying my best to get custody of you," he replied. Part of me wanted to get excited but even at this young age, looking around his apartment, I knew no judge would ever approve this place and give him custody of me. Years later I learned from reading my file that he had already given up his rights and never accepted any help from the courts. Go figure. But in the moment, I was just happy to see my daddy and get to spend time with him. I hung out at his place for a couple of hours and around lunch time I was hungry. I told him that I needed to go back to the foster home. He told me that he would take me to the mall tomorrow to get me some new clothes.

I kept pinching myself as I walked back to the foster home. I did not know what to think or how to feel. But underneath all of those feelings, I had butterflies. I felt calm knowing that I had family near me even though I hadn't seen him often. Before my dad got addicted to drugs, I remember a very different man. He would let me sit in his lap, steer the car and pretend that I was driving. I remember the old school red and yellow Fisher-Price car he got me for my birthday and how he pushed me down the streets in it. That man was very different than the man that just gave me a hug.

The next day, I skipped breakfast and went directly to my dad's apartment. I went to the side of the house to look up at the window that I had seen him in before, but the curtain was drawn. I went up to the porch and knocked on the door. I stood there for a couple of minutes before knocking again. I was reassuring myself that he was home while fighting back the tears making their way to my eyes. I stood there for a few more minutes looking at the peeling paint, trying to distract myself but who was I kidding? I knew he was a crackhead and wasn't reliable so why did I think he would keep his word? I turned to leave, upset at myself for actually thinking that he was telling the truth. I stepped off the porch and I heard the door open behind me.

My dad was standing there at the door. His eyes had tiny red veins in the white area, and he looked like he had just woken up. He motioned for me to follow him up the narrow stairs. Once I got to the top of the stairs, there was a hallway to a large room that looked like a living room. It was really messy and the air was thick with the smell of cigarettes. There were several people passed out on the floor or on couches. My dad told me to sit on a chair and to wait for him to get ready.

Once he walked out of the room, I hopped down from the chair and crept around the room trying not to wake anyone. There were alcohol bottles everywhere and the ashtrays were overflowing with butts. Aside from the party mess, the overall apartment was gross. The carpet was spotted with large stains in all different colors. The people asleep in the apartment were no better off. Most of them had open sores on their faces and bodies. The large leather couch had several people asleep on it and the arms of it were torn. There was several needles with the caps off on the coffee table. I was use to needles because my mom was a diabetic. I had seen her inject insulin twice a day into her belly for most of my life.

I went to reach for the needle on the coffee table when one person on the couch started to wake. It startled me and I tiptoed as fast as I could back to the seat where my dad told me to sit. I could hear my heartbeat in my ears as I tried to calm my breathing. A little while after, my dad walked into the living room. He looked a lot better than he did after he showered. He actually kinda looked like my dad before he started all the drugs and stuff.

He grabbed my hand and led me out of the apartment, and boy was I excited. It had been so long since I had seen my dad, let alone have a day with him. When we got to the street, the morning sun was moving to the middle of the sky and the brisk air was warming. I asked my dad, "Where are we going?" As I asked, I started skipping with excitement. He told me "We are going to the mall to get you a new outfit." I really didn't care where we were going as long as I was with my dad. On the walk to the mall, I thought about everything that had happened since that day when we were taken away. So much had happened to me in so little time. Yet, now as I held my dad's hand and walked down the street with the sun kissing my face, I had no worries in the world.

I really don't remember the walk to the mall but we stopped at Foot Locker once we got there. My dad let me pick out a new pair of Nikes and a matching outfit. I was giddy with excitement. I skipped halfway home. I asked my dad if we could stop at the corner store and get candy and pop. He smiled and shook his head yes. I slowly forgot that I was still in foster care for a minute and I just lived in this moment. We got candy and pop and my dad got some beer for himself. He cracked it open and joined me drinking while we walked down the street. He walked me up to the foster home's porch and told me to come over to his apartment later. I gave him a huge hug around his stomach. That was the first time I noticed that he wasn't as big as I remembered. He was always on the skinny side but very handsome with strong facial features. As a kid he seemed so large but now he wasn't. Was it that it had been so long since I had hugged him that I had grown much larger? None of that mattered anymore. I had my dad back.

I went inside and up to my bedroom. Jamal was already there laying down on his bed. I got undressed and put on my new outfit. He was eyeing me while I got dressed and I got butterflies in my stomach. I haven't felt like that since I had a sleepover at Cody's house. I stood there for a second with my leg halfway out of my pants. My mind wandered to Cody and the butterflies flew into my throat and formed a knot. I missed him and I could feel the tears swelling in my eyes, but I forced them down, knowing Jamal doesn't like to see people cry. I pulled my pants off and quickly pulled my new Nike basketball shorts on with the matching jersey. Jamal didn't avert his eyes the entire time. He did ask where I got my shoes and outfit from. "Footlocker," I told him. He asked me if I stole it. I quickly said no and told him I got it from Nonya.

"Nonya?" Jamal asked acting like he didn't know the saying.

"Yeah" I said, "None of ya business is where I got it from."

Jamal laughed and hopped down from his bed. He didn't ask any more questions and left the room. I finished tying my shoes and went downstairs. Most of the kids were in the living room watching *Speed Racer*, and I could hear others outside playing. The older kids were on the porch smoking cigarettes. That meant Foster Mom was at the casino and wouldn't be back for a while. One of the older girls who I really never even spoke to asked me where I got my stuff from. I ignored her, not wanting to tell her that I spent the day with my dad and that he bought it for me. But I also was afraid to give her the same smart ass response I gave Jamal. She came into the living room and asked me again. I shrugged my shoulders and backed into the hallway.

She ran up to me and grabbed me by my throat, "Did you steal this shit? You stole it didn't you?"

I panicked and I bit her hand and she dropped me, screaming and cursing at me. "This little faggot fucking bit me," she said.

She kept screaming while all the other kids came to look at the commotion. I stood up and looked at her, not knowing what I should do. I started backing down the hallway. She looked up at me and charged down the hallway, pushing me off of my feet. She pushed me so hard I flew down the hallway and hit the back of my head on a corner of the wall really hard. Instantly, I was filled with rage and jumped up to fight back. As I was making my way towards her, her face changed from rage to shock. It all happened so quickly. The other kids scattered like they had done before. I felt liquid dripping onto my shoulder and rolling under the Chicago Bull's jersey tank top. I looked down at my Nikes and blood dripped onto them. I reached behind my head and instantly felt the salt from the sweat on my fingers sting a huge cut in my head. The adrenaline of being mad faded and my body realized the cut on my head. I felt it and it hurt badly.

The girl yelled for Jamal, asking him to hurry and grab some bandaids as if they would stop the blood now pouring out of my head. I stood there in a haze. The other kids in the house seemed to be moving around me in slow motion. I kept looking down at my new Nikes that my dad had just bought me, which were now covered in my blood. The room began to spin, and I felt like I was going to pass out. I felt so lost in that moment, I let out an ear-piercing scream and ran out of the house covered in blood. I ran as fast as I could down the street and pounded on my dad's front door. No one came to the door at first. I stood there screaming and pounding my bloody fist on the door, soaking the peeling paint. I couldn't hear the footsteps of the person on the other side of the door or hear them unlock the bolt. I almost lost my balance when the door suddenly opened. It wasn't my dad. It was a skinny lady in a skimpy dress. Her eyes were bloodshot and she had scars on her arms. She was clearly high on that shit but seemed to sober up a little bit when she noticed the blood everywhere. She screamed for my dad and I saw him come from the top of the stairs. His eyes were also bloodshot, and he wasn't walking very well.

"What the fuck happened to your shoes?" he asked. I ran up to him to hug him and he pushed me back saying he didn't want blood all over him. He turned me around to look at the cut in my head. "You are going to need stitches little nigga." He ran upstairs leaving me there. I tried to stop my tears and catch my breath. A few seconds later, my dad came running down the stairs with a towel in his hand. He wrapped the towel around my head and told me the ambulance was coming.

The fire department arrived first and they removed the towel. I heard them all wince at the sight of the cut. They started putting gauze around my head, and then they loaded me into the ambulance. We got to the hospital and I went straight to the back. Everyone was making a fuss about my head and kept asking me if I felt sleepy. I told them I wasn't. I heard the doctor tell my dad that the cut was too large and too deep for stitches. They would have to use staples to close the cut. I started to panic at the thought of having huge staples in my head. One of the nurses came to calm me down and offered to get me a popsicle. I sat there enjoying my popsicle while the doctor used clippers to cut the hair around my cut. He had already numbed the area and gave me some pain meds, so I was in a much better mood then when I arrived. The staples weren't as bad as I thought they would be. And I was happy that the cut was closed. The doctor told my dad I was good to go home, and that I should take it easy for a two weeks. The doctor let us know the staples would need to be taken out by a doctor in a couple weeks. When the doctor mentioned that I would have to come back was the first time I had thought about the foster home. I wondered if Foster Lady even knew that I had gotten hurt. I chuckled to myself. I knew that she was most likely at the casino and if she was home the kids probably didn't even to bother to tell her what happened.

My dad checked me out with the nurse and we went to the lobby. I asked, "How are we going to get back?" My dad seemed agitated at the question but let me know that he was going to call my mom. My mom? I hadn't even thought about her. In fact, I was still upset at her for cancelling all those visits. But, I was still super excited to see her. I sat in the lobby while my dad went to find a payphone.

As I was sitting there, I thought about the last time I had been to the hospital. Funny enough, my dad had taken me then too. I rubbed the seven-inch scar that ran down my left leg, remembering the moment the accident happened. My mom had dropped my siblings and I off at our grandma's house in Detroit. It was only supposed to be for one night, but my mom had a habit of dropping us off and leaving us there for a couple of days at a time. We wouldn't hear from her at all.

One night while we were there, my grandma asked me to help dry the dishes. I loved helping but I was only five years old and really short so I had to pull up one of her old dining room chairs. I pushed the chair against the counter, right under the sink. And I climbed up and started drying the clean dishes. Jatia was washing the dishes and handing them to me to dry. I guess I got too excited because I started jumping up and down on the chair. The seat on the chair broke and I fell through the chair. I instantly felt a sharp sting on my leg. I looked down and Jatia started screaming for my grandma. I had cut my leg open and the cut was so deep I could see my bone and a couple veins pulsing. I've always had a high pain tolerance, so I didn't immediately freak out. I was just more grossed out at the sight of it.

My grandma ran into the kitchen, of course, more pissed about her broken dining room chair then the huge cut in my leg. My grandma wasn't always there mentally. She had years of heavy alcohol use and a mental disability, which was passed on to my mother who spent part of her child-hood in a mental hospital for suicidal thoughts. My grandma never made the right decisions. Jatia told grandma that I needed to go to the hospital. My grandma replied that I wasn't Jatia's responsibility. And our mom needed to come back, get us and take me to the hospital herself. She did disinfect the cut with peroxide and wrapped a couple of feminine pads around my leg securing them with tape, making a makeshift bandage. She gave me a couple of Tylenol and told me to go to sleep. My leg hurt but I ended up falling asleep. I woke up in the middle of the night with the worst pain, but I forced myself back to sleep not wanting to anger my grandma. I guess I went into shock before morning because I woke up in the hospital with my dad next to me. He really did love me. At least, I remember he did before the streets and the drugs got to him.

I snapped back after hearing my mom's voice getting loud at the hospital check-in counter. My dad grabbed my hand and led me over to her. She was wearing tight blue jeans with a white top. I noticed her outfit because I thought it was cute with her gold dolphin hoops and fresh white Adidas. Her complete look - from her finger waves hairstyle to her shoes – looked brand new. My mom turned around and immediately started yelling at my dad. She grabbed my hand and started walking with me towards the door. My dad followed us out of the hospital trying to reason with my mom. I couldn't hear a lot of what they were saying because my mom had put me inside of a car and walked away a little bit. I could hear her say, "He is staying with me." And from the gestures and the look on my dad's face I could tell that he knew he wasn't going to win this fight. He walked over to the passenger door and knelt down to look me in my eyes. I hugged him as hard as I could. Something in my gut told me that this might be the last time I see my father. He told me that I had to go with my mom, to be good, and that he loved me. He gave me one last hug and shut the door. My mom started the car and pulled off. I watched my dad get smaller and smaller in the rearview mirror until he disappeared. I didn't know it then, but it would be eighteen years before I saw him again -- at the funeral for my mom and sister.

20

Momma Comes Back

In the car, my mom immediately started asking me so many questions about what happened. "Where are you living? Did the foster person do this to you? Why did you find your father instead of looking for me?" The questions were nonstop. And when I couldn't answer the question fast enough or the right way in her mind, she yelled more. She was so different than what I remembered and certainly not how I imagined she would treat me when she saw me. I managed to ask a couple of questions of my own. "Where are we going? Are you taking me back to the foster home?"

Being alone with her was awkward. As the youngest of four, I was never alone with her even when she was even at home. She didn't answer any of my questions. Instead, she turned on the radio and we continued to drive.

We drove back to our house. I don't know why I was shocked that she still lived there. I guess I thought she moved because she wasn't there when we stopped by in the Child Haven bus a while ago. We pulled into the driveway and went up to the porch. I got sick to my stomach. This was the same spot where it all happened. It's where Tim and I convinced Jatia to open the door and the SWAT team came in with Miss Jennifer. The inside of the house was much different. In fact, she had boxes packed and most of the furniture was gone. I asked her why everything was packed up? Of course, she blamed my siblings and myself for having to move. She lost her Section 8 housing after we were taken and put into foster care. She told me that she was going to take me to Detroit, and we would live with grandma, which I wasn't very excited about. The only room in the house that still had furniture was my mom's bedroom. When I went inside the first thing I noticed was her mini fridge that was already locked and filled with drugs. She used to tell us it was just her insulin. After my dad robbed us that one time, I noticed that at night people would walk up to her window on the side of the house and she would give them drugs out of the mini fridge. So, at a very young age I knew she was a drug dealer. Sometimes, it was so obvious.

I remember before we were taken, we were headed back to Muskegon from Detroit. Deon, my mom's boyfriend, was driving with my mom in the passenger seat. All four kids were in the back seat of Deon's Cadillac. We were driving down the highway when all of a sudden there were blue and red lights flashing behind us. My mom quickly took a plastic bag of drugs and turned to the back seat and told Jatia to put them in her underwear. My sister shook her head and started to cry. My mom explained that that officers couldn't search a little girl's private area and that she would be okay. But if Jatia didn't do it, she would go to jail. "You don't want your mom do go to jail, do you?" she asked.

As Deon slowed the car down and pulled over, my mom gave the drugs to Jatia and she put them into the front of her underwear. I wish I could say that the traffic stop was routine but it was not. The officers ended up asking all of us to get out of the car to search it. They searched my mom and Deon and put them into the back of police cars. Then, they walked my siblings and I to the side of the highway on a grassy knoll. As we were walking, I held Jatia's hand tightly, afraid they would search her too. Thankfully, they didn't. They finished searching the car and released my mom and Deon.

Shortly after, we were back on the road. After my mom thought the coast was clear, she asked Jatia for the baggie back. Jatia gave it back to her. My mom laughed with Deon, bragging how they had outsmarted the police.

That first night staying with my mom was not anything like I had imagined all of those nights I laid awake crying for her in a strange foster home. I imagined all of my siblings in the house and a lot of laughter. Instead, it was just me laying down on my mom's bed, alone in a dark room. The light from the living room peeped through the slit of the door. My mom had told me she was having a little get together and I was to stay in the bedroom. I fell asleep listening to the voices coming from the other side of the door, trying to imagine what the faces looked like.

Suddenly, I heard a crash that sounded like breaking glass. I opened my eyes and it was pitch black, I rubbed them thinking maybe I was in a dream. My vision focused on the light underneath the door and I saw shadows moving. I heard screaming and cursing. And I jumped out of the bed and ran to the door. I cracked it open a little bit to peek my head out. I saw my mom standing at the front door with a gun in her hand. I am not sure who was outside but from the sound of it, they were ready to fight and maybe also had weapons. I opened the door and ran to my sister's room, closed the door and hid in a corner. All of her stuff was gone and the room was empty, but for some reason I still felt safe in there. The screaming continued for a while then it calmed down and I heard the front door slam shut. Whoever was there was gone now, and my eyes were getting heavy. I felt safer in my sister's room anyway, so I decided to stay in there.

I fell asleep. When I woke up it was morning time and the house was quiet. I went into the living room and there were beer bottles and aluminum foil tossed everywhere. Everyone was gone. My mom's door to her room was locked, which it usually was even if she wasn't home. I walked around the house, which was just a shell of itself now. So many memories came back to me. Some memories were good like the Christmas we had before my mom got addicted to her supply. Memories of seeing my favorite movies for the first time in the living room. I walked to the screened in porch where we used to keep our dog, Goldie, who was a Golden Shar Pei. We didn't have her for long because someone stole her. This was just a house now. It was no longer my home.

I sat on the porch until my mom woke up. She seemed shocked that I was on the porch, like she didn't remember what had happened the day before. Her eyes were heavy and bloodshot, but she seemed to be in a better mood. She came up to me, kneeled down and kissed my forehead and hugged me. As soon I felt her embrace, I completely broke down in tears, releasing every emotion I had kept in since we were taken away. By this point, it had been over a year of living from foster home to foster home. And I was so tired. I was tired of being strong, tired of being okay with being the scapegoat for my siblings. They all blamed me for telling Miss Chimney and bringing Miss Jennifer and the police to the house. I released all of the tears from the nights I cried myself to sleep wishing for my mom. Being held in her arms was like being held by a ghost, someone you grieved, someone who had died in your eyes. And yet here we were standing on the porch, the last place I stood before my life changed forever.

That day I helped my mom finish packing the house and loading the U-Haul. I built up enough courage to ask her what had happened to our stuff since we never got to take it to foster care with us. "I sold everything I could. And I gave the rest to your auntie so your cousin could use it," she answered. I rolled my eyes and let a frown settle on my face. I was really upset that she would sell our stuff, like we were never going to use it again. That was the first time that I thought about the idea of not going back home. If she was moving to Detroit, were we all moving there after she got us out of foster care? I tried to calm my brain down and not to overthink it, but I had a feeling that I would never be with my siblings again.

We were almost finished moving everything when there was a heavy knock on the front door. I was in the kitchen eating a bologna sandwich with a mini bag of Doritos when my mom came running into the kitchen and told me to get into the pantry. I didn't think twice and got into the pantry ducking under the lower shelf hiding myself as best as I could. My mom closed the pantry door and I heard her footsteps walk away. I was so freaking scared. I thought that maybe the people from the night before had come back with their own guns and there would be a shootout. I couldn't hear anything at first, so I put my ear under the crack in the door. I heard my mom talking to someone but couldn't discern what she was saying. Then, I heard the front door open and shut and footsteps walking around the house. I heard my mom asking why they were there and what happened to her kids. I was shocked when I heard Miss Jennifer's voice tell my mom that I was missing from the foster home I had been placed in. My mom pretended to be so upset about the news. She told Miss Jennifer that none of her kids ever went missing when she had us. She went on to say that she was going to sue the State for losing her child and that she wanted her other kids back. Miss Jennifer told her that there was evidence that I was taken to the hospital by my father. She asked my mom if she had seen my father in the last two days. "No," she said and continued to yell at Miss Jennifer about losing her youngest child. I heard their voices fade away again and the front door shut.

A moment afterward the pantry door opened and my mom told me to hurry up and that we needed to go. We waited a couple of minutes as my mom finished up cleaning and locking the house for the last time. I stood in the middle of the empty living room looking at the corner where I stood a little over a year ago, scared and confused as the police searched our house, took us away and put us into foster care. At this point, I didn't know what the future held but I was ready for anything.

I jumped into the front seat of the U-Haul and my mom started it and we left. We drove through the streets that I used to play in with my siblings. We passed the candy lady's house, who had the best and cheapest candy and all the neighborhood kids went to it. We rode past the school. I looked for Miss Chimney's class but couldn't tell which windows were hers. This was my neighborhood - the place where I had most of my childhood memories. My mom told me that we had to make one more stop before we headed to Detroit.

A couple minutes later we pulled up to my Auntie Paulette's house and went inside. My auntie was waiting for us in the kitchen with a worried look on her face. My mom asked her, "Why do you look so worried?" My auntie told her that my dad had called her and told her the police came to his house after they found out that he took me to the hospital. He told them that she had me, and he had no idea where she had taken me. My mom told auntie about my social worker, Miss Jennifer, coming by the house and looking for me, but she didn't find me so we were probably okay. They talked for a while. I watched *The Golden Girls* show on my auntie's TV.

They started yelling at each other and I heard my aunt say, "You are going to go to jail Mia." And my mom went quiet. I got up and listened to what they were saying. My aunt was telling my mom that if she didn't turn me back to the state, she would be on the run for felony kidnapping. Kidnapping? How could my own mother be charged with kidnapping? I was her son. I was so confused. And I was worried that my mom would give me back to Jennifer and I would go back to foster care. Or even worse, I'd go back to the Foster Lady's house full of those kids. I didn't want to go back. I wanted to go to Detroit with my mom. My mom started to cry, and I heard my auntie comfort her but sternly told her that she had to give me back. I ran back to the living room, trying to hold back my tears not knowing what my mom would do.

We got back into the U-Haul and started driving again. I was too nervous to ask my mom where we were headed because I really did not want to know the answer. I looked out the window and watched the city pass by. Tears started falling down my cheeks as I recognized where we were headed. If we were going to Detroit, we would be headed towards the highway. Instead, we were headed downtown towards the courthouse. I keep telling myself to calm down and that we were just headed a different way. When my mom pulled into the courthouse parking lot, I broke down. I screamed at the top of my lungs and threw my legs and arms everywhere in a fit. I keep screaming "why" and my mom just cried and tried to hold me as I threw a fit. She just sat there in that truck and held me as my world came crashing down again. After a while, she looked me in my eyes and told me that she was going to take me straight to the judge and show him the staples in my head. She told me that she was hoping that the judge would allow her to keep me because of the abuse I experienced in foster care. She said that she was starting the parenting classes and soon she would get my siblings back too. But first, we had to talk to the judge.

I calmed down enough to catch my breath and agreed to go speak to the judge with her. We walked into the Muskegon County Courthouse. I held my mom's hand tight as we walked down the beige halls. I hated courthouses. Nothing good ever happens at them, only sadness and tickets. There were wooden benches lined up against the walls in the hallway. My mom sat me on one and went up to the secretary's window. She was explaining the situation and asked to speak to the judge directly. She came back and told me that the judge was going to see us soon. She seemed more confident than she did in the truck and hoped that he would let her keep me. A couple minutes later a bailiff came to one of the doors and called my mom's name. I took her hand and we walked into the judge's chambers. There was so much wood everywhere - wooden walls, wood furniture and hundreds of books on the wooden shelves. Inside of the office there was another little sitting area with a couple of chairs. There was a large wooden door that must have been the judge's quarters. In the little waiting room, there was a small rectangular window that looked over the courthouse parking lot. I could see the U-Haul truck. It looked like a little toy from this high up. I was looking out of the window when I heard them call my mom's name. I got up and went to grab my mom's hand but the bailiff told my mom that the judge wanted to talk to her first alone. The secretary gave me some crayons and a coloring book. I sat there and colored waiting for my mom to come and get me. I didn't know how long it had been, but I had perfectly colored in several pages and my legs were falling asleep. I heard a door open and I looked up and saw Miss Jennifer. I immediately ran to the window and when I looked down at the parking lot, the U-Haul truck was gone.

I just stood there and looked out of the window numb. I had no more tears to cry. I felt abandoned and this time I knew she left me on purpose. I promised myself that I would never cry again for her. She could have taken me to Detroit, but she went by herself. As I write this book as an adult, I realize that my mother did the right thing. However, as that little boy standing in that room, I didn't understand.

21

Same Street, Different Shit

At the courthouse, I begged Miss Jennifer to not take me back to the foster home with the casino lady. I showed her the staples in my head and told her the story about what happened. I told her everything from my dad taking me to the mall to get my birthday outfit to my mom picking me up and taking care of me. Of course, I left out the guns and drug use. I wanted to show Miss Jennifer that my parents were good people and could take care of my siblings and me. Miss Jennifer really didn't seem like she was paying attention. She grabbed my hand and started walking out of the courthouse.

We drove to Catholic Social Services and Miss Jennifer parked in the employee parking lot in the back of the building. We walked into the building and I took a seat in the lobby while Miss Jennifer went to her office. I didn't know where I was going. I was just really hoping that it wasn't back to Child Haven. I was sitting in the lobby counting the number of tiles on the ceiling, something I do when I am nervous. I was busy counting when the front door opened and I looked and saw a familiar face. It was Lindsey! She was walking with a little toddler holding her hand. She saw me and recognized me, which made me special for a moment. She came up to me, gave me a hug and rubbed my head. She didn't say anything, but she didn't need to. By the way she held that little boy, I knew he was the one who got adopted. I was just the cute, troubled black kid from the inner city. But still, I was happy for her happiness.

Miss Jennifer called for me from the door by the reception window. I walked up and went into the office area. To the right of the office was the family visiting rooms. I had been there before, but our visits always got cancelled. To the left of the visiting room, there were tons of cubicles with computers, decorations, drawings and pictures on the wall. Past the cubicles, there was a staircase where there were more cubicles and large conference rooms. Miss Jennifer's cubicle was upstairs. Unlike the ones downstairs, her cubicle was not decorated and she didn't have anything on the wall. There were lots of folders on her desk that were stuffed full of papers. I sat in a chair next to her desk and she asked me if I was okay. I shook my head yes and asked her where I was going next. "I really don't know at the moment, but we will make sure you have somewhere to sleep tonight," Miss Jennifer replied. I said, "I hope so," while looking down on the ground. She then said that if she couldn't find a placement home, I would have to go back to Child Haven until she found a foster home. I didn't even want to think about that option. So, I put all of my hope in Miss Jennifer finding a home for me today.

A few hours later, I was in the back seat of her red Pontiac again. She had found a foster home for me. We drove for about twenty minutes and pulled onto a street that I was actually familiar with. It was the same street that the Beasleys lived on. Miss Jennifer pulled into a driveway of a nice brick, two-story home with a well-manicured, fenced-in front yard. I asked Miss Jennifer if she knew that the Beasleys lived down the street and reminded her how they had beat me up before. I knew my sister wasn't still living with them at this point, so I was afraid. Regardless, it was better than Child Haven.

We went to the front door and rang the doorbell. I heard a voice come from the other side of the door, "Hold on" the voice said. When the door opened there was a large Native American lady, at least six feet tall and she looked like she was in her seventies. She was wearing a large muumuu that stopped right below her knee. I saw part of false leg on the right side. She introduced herself and told me I could call her Bigsy. She invited Miss Jennifer and I inside and told us to follow her. I noticed that she walked with a limp, probably because of her false leg. We followed her into the house and passed a living room with a big chandelier and all of the furniture was covered in plastic. You could tell that no one used this room and it was just for show. We walked to the back of the house. There was a large kitchen with an emerald green wall and wood cabinets with a huge wooden table in the middle. There were copper cake molds on the walls as decoration and a bathroom right next to it. Ms. Bigsy opened a door that was next to the bathroom, and there were steps leading up. She told me to go up and check out my room while she talked to Jennifer. I grabbed my garbage bag full of clothes and took them upstairs. The room was a converted attic that was the size of the whole house. There was a couch with a TV in the front of the room. And in the back of the room, there were two beds with a dresser between them along the wall. It was one of the nicest rooms I had slept in ever. I sat on one of the beds, looked at the room and took in my surroundings. I could hear the muffled voices of Miss Jennifer and Ms. Bigsy. I set my bag of clothes on the other bed and went downstairs to say goodbye to Miss Jennifer. She was sitting at the kitchen table showing Ms. Bigsy some paperwork. I went into the bathroom that was next to the attic door. The bathroom had wall-to-wall mirrors, even the sink cabinet was made of mirrors. The toilet was emerald green that matched the large jet bathtub sitting next to it. I sat down to pee and looked at the tub. I was really excited to take a bath in it. I had never been in a jet jacuzzi tub before. I thought about all the bubbles I would make with the water jets and soap.

I didn't let myself get too excited. I don't even know if she will even let me use the tub.

There was a knock on the door and Miss Jennifer let me know that she was headed out. I finished and went out to say goodbye, but Miss Jennifer had already left. Ms. Bigsy was still sitting at the table. She asked if I was hungry. I shook my head yes and took a seat at the table.

She heated up some catfish that she pulled from the fridge. The fish was so good and salty. I knew that I would love her cooking. I finished and asked if I could go outside. She shook her head yes. I walked out of the large brick house and looked down the street. I knew this neighborhood. The Beasely house was at the end of the street. I started walking down the street and saw a bike leaning up against the side of the house. I looked around to see if anyone was watching. With the coast being clear, I took the bike and went for a joyride. I would bring it back when I was done. Plus, it didn't look like anyone was using it. I rode the bike around the neighborhood, getting myself familiar again. I passed the candy lady's house where she sold candy to the neighborhood kids. I headed to the field that all the kids play tackle football in. There was a game going on and I recognized a couple of the players. I saw Anton and Juan Beasely. I was far enough away that they wouldn't see me or so I thought. Juan saw me and started yelling something. I turned my bike around and started pedaling away. I got a couple of feet before I felt something hit me in the back of the head making me lose my balance and run into a curb. I fell off the bike scraping my knee. I heard all of the kids laugh and looked at the bike. The wheel was completely bent. Juan yelled out that I was a faggot and the group started laughing again. I picked up the bike and started pushing it back. As I was pushing the bike back, I started to worry about getting into trouble. I assured myself that no one would even know it was me. I thought, even though I did take the bike from the neighbor's yard, they didn't know me. I pushed the bike down the street and I saw Ms. Bigsy watering her grass. I tried to rush past her. She saw me and yelled for me to come to her.

"What did you do to my granddaughter's bike?" she asked. I stood there confused. Who was her granddaughter? I lied and said I found it on the street. She looked at me like she didn't believe me. She told me to follow her as she crossed the street. I pushed the bike as I followed, still confused about what was going on. We got to the house across the street where I had taken the bike. Ms. Bigsy walked up to the door opened it and went inside leaving me at the stoop with the bike. A few moments later she was back at the front door with a young girl my age.

"Is this your bike? And did you leave it outside on the street?" She asked. The girl shook her head no. Ms. Bigsy screamed at her, "Speak when I speak to you Pooh." Pooh said, "No ma'm," nervously and looked at me. Ms. Bigsy looked at me and asked if I lied to her. I didn't have the heart to lie in front of this little girl named Pooh. I told her I lied about finding the bike and told her I got it from the side of the house. She kissed Pooh on the head and sent her back into the house. Ms. Bigsy told me to put the bike back on the side of the house.

We walked back to the house and Ms. Bigsy told me to go around the back and to get a switch. I immediately started crying and shaking my head no. I threw myself on the ground in a fit and she left me, screaming at the top of my lungs and went into the house. I was there for what seemed like an hour, but it may have been only twenty minutes. I gathered myself together and went inside. I found Ms. Bigsy at the table waiting for me with a belt. She grabbed me by my wrist and put me along her leg. I remember being down by her leg because the artificial leg was a different color than the real leg. And I remember how it felt. Cold. She started giving me a whooping. At first I cried but she really wasn't hitting me hard. I had been hit harder, so I just let her finish hitting me. When she finished, she told me to go to my room. That was the first day at Ms. Bigsy's house and I fell asleep wondering how it would work out.

The next day, there were people downstairs and I saw the little girl, Pooh, who I had met the previous day. There were two other women there as well. One was really pretty and the other was really pretty but had a tomboy look. Ms. Bigsy introduced them as her daughters. She said that one was Pooh's mom. I don't remember her name, but the tomboy one's name was Cynthia. She let me know they owned all the houses on the block. There were only five houses. And I should think twice before I take anything from the houses on that block.

We had breakfast at the long table in the kitchen, and Ms. Bigsy told me to go get dressed because we were going yard selling. I loved going to yard sales because they usually had cheap toys. That day with her was actually really fun. And she seemed to be a nice lady unless you did something wrong, which seemed fair. As the days turned into weeks, I was enrolled into Nims Elementary school. Ms. Bigsy told the school that she did not think I needed special education and fought for me to not be in special ed. That was the first time since being with my mom in first grade that I was not in special ed. It was the beginning of my fourth grade year and things were pretty normal. I avoided the neighborhood kids though, and I played with Pooh often and had sleepovers. I played with her dolls and Barbies. Her mom seemed to have a problem with it because she was a Christian and didn't find it appropriate. But she came to understand it since it was no harm.

I became closer with Cynthia at this time. She was Ms. Bigsy's daughter who lived in one of the houses on the block. She said that she always wanted to adopt a boy like me and maybe in the future she would adopt me. I used to spend nights at her house, and we would stay up all night watching movies and eating popcorn. She would teach me how to clean and the proper way to clean the stove and floors. She would often say, "No matter who I was with, everyone wanted someone who could clean."

Ms. Bigsy also used to pay me for my chores around the house and would take me thrift shopping whenever her state check came in so that I could get new clothes. I really spent a lot of time getting to know everyone in this family, but everything wasn't perfect. I would often get in trouble, either at school, at home, or in the neighborhood. Ms. Bigsy would punish me by spanking me or locking me upstairs in the attic room.

One time, I was playing with Pooh and I pushed her down and she scraped her leg leaving a big scar. Ms. Bigsy got extremely mad at me. I don't understand exactly what happened. Ms. Bigsy's eyes rolled into the back of her head and she started speaking in a weird language - almost like a chant. While doing this, she burned some things and she put them in a tray. Then, the cabinets in the kitchen started opening and closing by themselves. I got scared and ran up to the attic room. I tried to turn on the lights, but none of them worked. The only light was the moonlight coming through the window. So, I moved my bed into the moonlight and crawled into it. Whatever she had said or done to me, I was scared and knew it was bad. That night I heard scurries and voices in my room that night. The next morning, she was in the kitchen cooking breakfast. She told me that until I came back and apologized for the disrespect that I had caused, everything in my life with potential would fail. I did eventually go back and apologize but it would be a decade later. That was all she said as she fed me my breakfast..

Months went by and I was doing well in school. I had even joined the basketball team. Ms. Bigsy would drop me off for my practice and games. During this time, I had begun visitation with my siblings. We would meet at Catholic Social Services or McDonald's. During those visits, I learned that my siblings were also doing well, except for my brother Alex. Jatia was doing well in her foster home with Ms. Hidleburg who had a big house in Muskegon Heights. Ms. Hidleburg's house looked very nice and she seemed really cool. One day I spent the day with her family, she had all foster girls who were preteens or teenagers. I knew this because one day I asked Ms.

Hidleburg if she could be my foster mom, but she said she did not foster boys. Nonetheless, my sister seemed happy.

After one visit, I remember Jennifer was dropping me off first and my sister off second because we lived close to each other. I was crying because I missed her and I missed my siblings. So, she gave me her purple see-through Nintendo Game Boy and told me to give it back when I saw her again. That Game Boy got me through a lot because it was more than just a game. It was a reminder that I had a family.

22

Surprise Goodbye Visit

A few weeks before Thanksgiving, I was at school and I got called to the office. I was nervous because I had not done anything wrong or been in any trouble. It was Miss Jennifer and she had come to take me out of school for a visit with my mom. I didn't know what to say. I was so excited. I hadn't seen her since the U-Haul drove away.

I don't remember the drive there, but I remember getting to Child Haven and running to the visitor room - half expecting it to be empty. But it wasn't, my mom was there with my sister and my two brothers. Her hair was gelled down and slicked back. She had on black-wired, round glasses, t-shirt and shorts. I'll always remember her smile because of the gap between her two front teeth. I ran up to her and gave her a huge hug and she hugged me back. I asked her where she had been. And she told me she moved to Detroit with my grandma and that she was working on going back to school and getting a job. She told us that everyone in the family was good. When I asked her when she was getting us back, she just changed the subject and would play games with us in the room. We played with different games for what felt like hours. We played with Yahtzee and Dominoes. We even ordered pizza! We had never had a visit like this before.

After we ate, we all took pictures on the couch in the visiting room. I had on blue shorts and a t-shirt. And I remember asking for one photo with my mom by herself. Miss Jennifer came in and told us that it was time to wrap up the visit and my mom started to cry. I asked my mom why she was crying. She didn't answer. She just gave me a kiss on my forehead and told me she was sorry. Seeing my mom cry got Jatia and Alex angry and they began yelling at Miss Jennifer, asking her what they had done to my mom. Chaos broke out. Security came in and escorted my mom out. Other case workers came in and started to separate the kids. In all the chaos, I saw the camera get thrown on the floor and I picked it up and put it in my pocket.

Miss Jennifer brought me to her office upstairs. In between my sobs, I asked her what had just happened. She gave me a tissue and told me to try to calm down. After I finished blowing my nose and stopped crying, she told me that was the last time I would be able to visit my mom. My mom had signed over her parental rights. After hearing her say this, I just heard ringing in my ears. The type of ringing where, you don't know where its coming from, but you couldn't make it stop. I didn't cry. I just asked to go back to Ms. Bigsy's house. Miss Jennifer asked if I was okay, and I told her that I would have to be. When I got back to Ms. Bigsy's house I asked her to develop the photos at the Walgreens up the street. She gave me the money to do it myself. I kept those photos in my forever shoebox. I never knew those were the last photos I would take with my mom as I was taking them sitting on her lap smiling.

23

Trick Bikes, Abuse and Peg Legs

Knowing that I would never see my mother again, I soon started misbehaving in school to the point where they had to put me in special ed part-time. Ms. Bigsy was not happy about that. I also started misbehaving more at home. And Ms. Bigsy started giving me harsher and harsher whoopings. One day, she said that I was evil and had to clean the evil spirit out of me. She put me in the tub with the jets that I loved so much. She filled it up with scalding, hot water and made me get inside. She then poured half a bottle of bleach into the water and turned on the jets. She started scrubbing my skin with a pumice stone. I screamed. She simply said this was how she would wash the evil out of me.

Ms. Bigsy also started to get into disagreements with Cynthia. When she would beat me or do harsh punishments, I would run over to Cynthia's house crying. Then, things overall went from bad to worse. At Christmas time, Ms. Bigsy got me my own bike. It was a trick bike with four pegs - the one I always wanted. She let me unwrap it and ride it once on the ice outside. Then, she told me to go and put it across the street in Pooh's garage because that was not my bike. Since I had wrecked Pooh's bike, I had to give her mine. The emotional and physical abuse by Ms. Bigsy continued and got worse as time went on. And I felt completely stuck and lost because I knew I would never go home to my mom.

One of my punishments was to rub her peg leg and I hated touching it because it looked like the end of hot dog. One day I did not want to rub her leg and I told her I did not want to do it. She told me to go get a belt. I stood up, said no and grabbed her peg leg from by the nightstand. I ran up to the attic. She hobbled to the end of the staircase but she was too heavy to hop up the stairs. I told her if she would not hit me I would give her the leg back. She hobbled away and went back to her room. A while later, I wandered downstairs and saw she was asleep, so I put her leg back near her nightstand.

Nothing much changed at Ms. Bigsy's. I tried to stay out her way and do my best in school. In the springtime, I was in the school library when I got called into the principal's office.

I was in the library in the springtime, before school got out, and I was called to the office. I prepared myself, waiting for the worst to happen. It was Miss Jennifer and she had two garbage bags full of my belongings. She told me she was there to take me to another foster home and would explain on the way there.

24

Millers, Pizza, & Pumping

I had been in the back of Jennifer's red Pontiac Grand Am so many times that I knew every detail of the car. From the large circular vents to the bright red, dashboard lights. I felt so lost and in despair. I asked Jennifer if I would have to switch schools again. At this point it really didn't matter because I never had time to make friends before I'm moved to another foster home. When I first went into foster care and would move homes, I would ask a thousand questions and worry about the foster parents. But now, I knew just to prepare myself for the worst-case scenario. If they were better than the scenario I expected then great, but usually they were the worst-case scenario.

The rest of the car ride was silent. I watched the city roll past me in a blur. We drove towards Lake Michigan. I loved the lake. The sand in the summertime was so hot that it would burn your feet if you walked slow barefoot. On a hot summer day, you would see people skipping around the beach trying not to burn their feet. The water was so amazing. It was not warm but also not so cold that you couldn't enjoy it for a couple hours in between making sandcastles. I loved how large and impossible Lake

Michigan appeared. We learned in school that a lake is a body of water surrounded by land. But, Lake Michigan is so large you can't see the other side of it even with binoculars. As a matter of fact, the other side of the lake was an entirely different state called Wisconsin. I have never been out of the state of Michigan so I'm not sure what it looks like on the other side. Even still, I do know I love the Lake.

Miss Jennifer parked on the street in front of a nice, two-story house with an attached garage. The house had white siding and black window shutters with a bright red door. There was a huge skateboarding halfpipe that took up the entire driveway. I saw three kids on top of the halfpipe, and one was skating on it. They all stopped and looked at me. I waved but none of them waved back. I shrugged my shoulders and followed Miss Jennifer to the front door. Before she could even knock, the door opened and an older white woman with graying, short blond hair greeted us. She smiled brightly as she welcomed us into the house. This house was much different from Mrs. Bigsy's house. It had a family feel. It was clean but you could tell that kids lived here as well. She introduced herself as Sharon and said that her husband Pat was at work and would be home after dinner time. She was a white woman in her mid-sixties. She wore wide-legged jeans and a nice blouse. She showed us around the house, starting with the formal living room. She said that space was for quiet time and homework. There was a large kitchen in the back of the house that looked out at the backyard. I saw there was a trampoline and I was excited to use it. She said the basement was a hangout for the boys and there were video games, TVs and toys to play with down there. She told Miss Jennifer that the older boys who were preteens and teenagers wanted their own space. She said it smelled like dirty socks down there so she never ventured down, except to do the laundry. She showed us the bedroom upstairs. There were two bedrooms with a bathroom that divided them. Sharon said the room to the right was her biological son's room. And the room on the left was the foster room. As I passed her son's room, I saw a flat screen TV with a new PlayStation 2 and nice beds with colorful bedding. She showed us the foster room and there were two sets of old wooden bunk beds with beige and brown sheets. There was an old tube TV with dials and a VCR sitting on a dresser with four drawers. The lower bunks were taken. I climbed up on the top bunk and laid down. Miss Jennifer said goodbye and went downstairs with Sharon. I heard them speak for a little bit then the front door opened and shut.

I must have fallen asleep because I opened my eyes and the TV was on. I looked over the bed railing and there was a black kid with big, brown eyes looking back at me. He said hi and told me his name was Joe. I told him my name and got down from my bunk. I had seen him skating with the other boys. We asked each other questions and found out we had a lot of similarities. We were the same age, and his birthday was a month before mine. Joe told me that he loved the beach and that it was in walking distance from the house. I was so excited about that. We talked and watched *The Adams Family* show until Sharon called us down for dinner.

I followed Joe downstairs to the kitchen and sat at the table with him. I smelled steak and onions. When I saw Sharon plating the food, my mouth started watering. I heard footsteps coming down the stairs and the two boys who were skating outside appeared. The taller one looked about fourteen or fifteen years old and had dark brown hair. He looked like one of the guys from the backstreet boys. The younger boy was my height with a blond, bowl cut with blue eyes. They didn't introduce themselves. They just came down into the kitchen and grabbed the plates that Sharon was making. They didn't sit with Joe and I either. Instead, they took their plates and went downstairs to the basement. The other two plates she wrapped up in aluminum foil and put in the warmer in the oven. I was confused for a second until she took out paper plates and put hotdog buns on them. I hadn't noticed the pot of boiling water on the stove. Sharon took a couple of hotdogs out of the water and placed them in the buns with chips. She sat the plates in front of Joe and I and asked if we wanted ketchup. I shook my head yes, half in disbelief. She surely wasn't going to serve the foster kids hotdogs while the rest of the family got steak. Yet, this was the reality of the situation and every meal I had afterwards with the Millers.

After dinner, Joe showed me the kid's room in the basement. It was a large basement that was split in two sections by the staircase. He told me that our space was on the right, which had a large, blue corduroy, sectional couch. There was a Nintendo 64, which reminded me of Cody and our sleepovers we had playing *Mario Kart* on his Nintendo. On the left side of the basement was Aaron's corner, Joe told me. We were only allowed over there if we were invited by Aaron. The rest of that first night we spent watching *That's So Raven* until Sharon called down and told us it was time to go to bed.

It was so weird waking up the next morning and getting ready for school in a whole different house but going to the same school. Every other time I switched foster homes I switched schools as well. I had become accustomed to it. But this time was different. This time, nothing changed except where I lived. Joe was already in the bathroom showering and we took turns getting dressed in the bedroom. We went downstairs for breakfast, which was cereal. I asked Joe if he went to Nim's Elementary school. He told me that he went to the school closer to the house. I was kind of bummed because I hoped that he went to my school. Nonetheless, I was excited to go to school. I wasn't in special ed anymore, thanks to Ms. Bigsy. I also was the chief crossing guard and hall monitor, which gave me special privileges. Kids picked on me for being a tattletale, but it was better than being made fun of for being a foster kid. I was finally happy with school.

The Millers were Catholic, which meant we spent a lot of time in church. Besides Mass, Sharon also volunteered at the food shelter on the weekends and would bring us to help out. On the ride home after a one long day of volunteering, Shawn, the youngest son, asked Sharon if they could order pizza. She said yes. I got excited and looked at Joe and he rolled his eyes. He had lived with the Millers long enough to know that foster kids were never fed the same as Aaron and Shawn. When we got home, Sharon called Papa Johns and ordered two large pizzas. I nudged Joe in excitement, indicating that maybe it was for us as well. He just looked to the ground. After Sharon got off the phone, she went into the pantry in the kitchen and then handed Joe and I each a packet of Ramen Noodles. My heart dropped but I was so hungry I didn't really care. I went into the kitchen and started warming up water. Joe and I cooked our Ramen Noodles on the stove.

As we were sitting at the table, the doorbell rang. Sharon paid for the pizza and placed the boxes on the table in front of Joe and I. It smelled so good that I tried not to look at it. Aaron came up from the basement and grabbed one of the pizzas and brought it downstairs for him and Shawn to share. Joe sat there with a blank look on his face, eating his hotdog. After we were finished eating, Joe went downstairs. It was my night to clean the kitchen and take out the trash. I didn't have much to clean up because they ordered pizza and used paper plates. Sharon had put the second pizza in the oven to keep it warm for her husband Pat. I never really saw him that much around the house, and he never went anywhere with us foster kids. He mostly worked. And when he got home, he would go to his room and watch hockey and play solitaire on his computer. I thought to myself, maybe I should take a piece of pizza. No one was in the kitchen. But I was too afraid of getting into trouble. Sharon wouldn't feed us at all if we got into trouble.

I walked downstairs and Aaron's side of the room was dark. Shawn was sitting on the couch watching TV on the foster side. I asked him if he had seen Joe and he shrugged his shoulders. I heard slapping noises coming from the laundry room, which was on Aaron's side of the basement. Shawn tried to tell me I couldn't go over there but I shushed him. The laundry room door was cracked and I peeked inside. I saw Joe bent over and Aaron was thrusting himself inside of him. I got scared and ran back to the foster side of the basement, jumped on the couch and pulled my knees to my chest. I had a knot in my throat, and I was shaking. I didn't know what to think or what to do. So, I did nothing. I just sat there and watched the *Suite Life of Zak and Cody*. Shawn turned the volume up to drown out the slapping and we looked at each other. I could tell that he knew what was going on and it scared him too.

After a while, Aaron came out of the laundry room. He turned on his TV and PlayStation, laid down on his couch and played video games. Joe had ran upstairs to the bathroom and came back down shortly with a paper plate. He walked over to Aaron and put his plate out in front of him and Aaron took a slice a pizza out of the box and put it on the plate. Joe came over to our side and sat down in front of the TV on the floor and ate his pizza. None of us said anything to each other the rest of the night.

Joe and I became very close and would hang out together a lot after school. We spent a lot of time sunbathing and making sandcastles on the beach. We did everything together. We even did those stupid school fundraisers where you sold stuff out of a magazine door-to-door. Even though we were super close, Joe never spoke about his time with Aaron in the laundry room. It occurred a couple of other times since the first instance, but Joe always acted like nothing happened. I didn't really push the issue too much either because I didn't want it to start happening to me.

25

Forever waiting for a Forever Home.

One fall afternoon, Joe and I were on the swings at the park and Shawn came down on his bike. He came to tell me that my social worker was at the house and that I needed to go home. I ran as fast as my legs would take me all the way back to the Miller's house, trying not to come up with worst-case scenarios in my head. I thought that maybe Miss Jennifer was there to take me to another foster home. Or worse, maybe she'd take me back to Child Haven. When I got back to the Miller's house, she told me I had to go with her to Catholic Social Services to do an adoption commercial. I was relieved to know that I was not going to another foster home. However, that worry switched to anxiety because this was the first time that the reality that I was up for adoption really set in.

We got to Catholic Social Services and there was a camera crew from the local news with lights and two chairs set up. Miss Jennifer took me to the visitation room with toys and Jatia was there as well. I was surprised to see Jatia. I ran up to give her a hug and she hugged me back. She asked me how I was doing and if I had a new foster home. I hadn't seen her since I was at Ms. Bigsy house and we had our last family visit. After we talked, we just sat there on the couch. I fiddled with some toys, and Jatia just sat there and sucked her thumb. It's what she did when she was nervous. So, we both just sat there, anxiously waiting for them to come and get us. We did not know what was about to happen or what they wanted us to say.

Miss Jennifer came to the playroom and brought us to the room where they were doing the interviews. I thought it was kind of cool when I saw all the lights and cameras. But when the lady started asking us questions about being adopted and wanting to be adopted, I got nervous. They asked me if I would like a "Forever Family." I told them that I would like one and I asked them if my siblings could come with me. The lady told me that, "Unfortunately, not all my siblings could come. But hopefully, we could each find our own 'Forever Family' and we could grow up and visit each other." She asked Jatia if she wanted a forever family, but Jatia told her no one would adopt her because she was too old. Jatia also said that she didn't want to replace her mom. And when she got out of foster care, she was going back to her mom and help get us back. The interviewer looked at Miss Jennifer and then Jennifer removed Jatia from the room. After Jatia left the room, the lady asked me more questions about what type of family I would like. I told her that I didn't mind, as long as they were nice and liked to travel because I wanted to travel the world and see new things. They asked me a few more questions and then the interview was over. Miss Jennifer took me back to the Miller's house.

26

lies and the law

A few weeks had passed since the adoption interview. Things were getting back to normal at the Miller's and I had not heard anything about the interview. Joe and I went down to the park where we normally played and we skated around the parking lot. Shawn and Aaron rode their bikes down to the park and joined a lot of kids who were there with us. Joe and I avoided the other kids at the park because they usually got in trouble and would vandalize a lot. We saw them talking to Aaron who pulled spray paint out of his backpack. They were building a new bathroom at the park and they were renovating other parts. We saw Aaron, Shawn, and a few other boys from the neighborhood go behind the bathroom building. Joe and I followed them to see what they were doing. We saw that they were using spray paint to vandalize the building.

After a while, we started walking back to the Miller's. Joe and I got back to the house and went downstairs to the basement to play video games. We were playing for about an hour before Shawn and Aaron came running downstairs and they seemed like they were in a panic. Aaron went to his side of the room. And Shawn came and hopped on the couch with Joe and I and acted like he had been there the whole time. A few moments later I heard the front doorbell ring. I heard voices at the front door and then heavy shoes walk across the living room. Shawn looked nervous and I looked over at Aaron, who had his feet kicked up on the couch and was playing *Grand Theft Auto*.

Sharon called us all upstairs. I went upstairs with Joe and there were two officers in the kitchen. The officers asked us all to sit down. Shawn, Aaron, Joe and I, all sat around the table. They let us know that the neighbors had seen us all at the park before the vandalism happened. Joe and I told them we had been there. Since we didn't want to be snitches, we let them know we didn't do it. Shawn said that he did not do anything. Aaron looked at the officers and told them it was Joe and I. The officers asked us where we got the paint from. Joe didn't say anything but looked at the ground. I told them it was not us, but it was Aaron's paint. Aaron did artwork and would paint skateboards. I told the officers that I watched him and the other neighborhood boys vandalize the building. I was nervous and scared to stand up for myself but I knew that if I had gotten in trouble with the police I was less likely to be adopted. Aaron said that I stole his paint and must have did the vandalism. Sharon chimed in and told the officers that Joe and I were both troubled foster kids and had been in trouble before. She said that her kids had never been in trouble. The officers told us they wanted to speak with each kid by themselves and find out the truth. They started with Joe and Sharon told the rest of us to go downstairs and wait until we were called. I started crying as I walked downstairs, and Aaron and Shawn were following me.

When we got downstairs, I went over to Aaron's side and asked him why he was lying. He chuckled and said, "Because I can." I started crying more and Aaron told me he could help me out, but I would owe him. I told him I wanted him to tell the truth, and he said he would. Shawn was called next and Joe came back downstairs, not saying anything and still looking down at the ground. Shawn was upstairs for a little bit and he came down, then they called Aaron.

We watched a whole episode of the *Suite Life* before Sharon called for us all to come upstairs. When we came upstairs the police were gone and Aaron was sitting at the table eating ice cream. Sharon told us that we were not allowed to hang out with the brothers from around the block who Shawn and Aaron had vandalized the bathroom with. She told me that I was in trouble for lying on Aaron and that she would handle that situation later. She then thanked Aaron for telling the truth and told him he was not allowed to hang out with those boys because they were a bad influence. Aaron said that he was sorry that he given them the paint and that he thought they were going to paint their skateboards. Sharon told me to go to bed for the evening and that I would not have dinner because of my lies. She told Joe to follow me because he also did not tell the truth.

Sharon did not feed us anything but bread and water for the next three days. And we were not allowed to use the basement playroom and were quarantined to our room. Joe and I did not really mind because we knew that we told the truth. And we still had the old TV with a couple of channels in the room. We just watched black and white movies all day.

The first Saturday that we were allowed to use the basement room, it was around 8 a.m. and Sharon and Pat were still asleep. We were not allowed to make any noise or eat breakfast until they got up. Joe and I went downstairs to the playroom and watched TV by ourselves for an hour or so before Aaron came down. He came and sat down on the foster side and asked what we were watching. Neither of us said anything. He then told us that the brothers from down the street were probably going to "juvie" for the vandalism. He asked us if we were glad that it wasn't us who was going to juvie. He said that foster kids that go to juvie usually end up in prison and don't get adopted. He looked at me and said that it would be a shame if I went to juvie and messed up my chances of getting adopted. I still did not say anything but tears just welled up in my eyes and I continued to look at the screen. He asked us if we were hungry. We shook our heads no, but we both knew we were starving. We had not eaten anything but bread and water for the past three days.

Aaron went upstairs and came down with a box of blueberry muffins, the prepackaged ones from the big warehouse stores. Those were locked up in the cabinet, but he must have had a key or knew where the key was. He asked us if we wanted one. Joe got up and got one for himself. Seeing Joe eat the blueberry muffin I went and got one myself. Aaron told Joe to go to the laundry room and he told me to go follow him in there as well. I shook my head no and told him I did not want to do that. And he told me fine, and that when his mom and dad got up he was going to tell them that he felt bad for me because I was a foster kid, but it was me that did the vandalism. I begged him not to tell because I wanted to get adopted. The familiar knot came back to my throat and I couldn't say anything.

So, I went into the laundry room where Joe was already waiting. Aaron followed me and closed the laundry room door and pulled down his pants. He took advantage of Joe and I that morning, but I wish I could say that he had taken my innocence - that was already taken by Deon. I went back to my safe place, a place where I could not get hurt and what happened to me physically would not happen to me in my imaginary place. Joe and I never told Sharon in fear that she would not believe us, and we would end up in juvie because Aaron would tell her we did the vandalism. The abuse happened for months and got progressively worse. Aaron only stopped sexually abusing me when I bled for three days one time, and Sharon found blood in my underwear while she was doing laundry. She asked me why there was blood in my underwear. I told her I had diarrhea and there was blood in my stool. She believed me but I got in trouble for wasting underwear.

Life at the Miller's got progressively worse. Miss Jennifer would call and check on me and Sharon would tell her that I was out at the beach or out playing with the boys. In reality, I was locked in the room or downstairs in the basement with Aaron. My butt hurt so bad that I could not sit still at school. And I thought to myself that maybe going to juvie was better than staying with the Millers.

27

Forever Family

On my walk home from school, a few weeks before Thanksgiving break, I thought that I should say something to Miss Jennifer or the teachers about Aaron's sexual abuse. I walked up the street to the Miller's and Miss Jennifer's red Pontiac Grand AM was parked in the driveway. All the anxiety that I had been fighting came back to me and I told myself that juvie was okay. I told myself not to cry. I walked through the door and Miss Jennifer was sitting in the living room with Sharon and a stack of books. They were large books like photo albums. Miss Jennifer looked happier than her normal self and asked me how was school. I told her I had a good day and asked her why she was here. She said that a family was interested in adopting me and had left photo albums for me to look through. And if I like the photos and their family, then they would love to come meet me at the Miller's. I asked her what was their names. And she was told me, Sean and Debbie Gum. I asked her what the books were. She told me they were the scrapbooks of the family that Debbie made. She told me she had met them, and they were very nice people. She told me that they had a son of their own. He was six months older than me and named Christopher. They lived in a big house in the woods. Jennifer told me she would leave the books with me for a while and that she would come back to see what I thought about meeting them. I was so excited, but I did not want to show it. I took the books and went up to my room.

Joe was already on his bunk and I told him that I might get adopted. Joe said congratulations and that he was happy for me. He said that I better make it happen fast before Aaron makes it not happen.

That night I looked through the scrapbooks and I saw a white family who looked really happy. The dad was tall with brown hair and a beard. The mom was average looking with curly brown hair and bangs. And their son, Christopher, had brown hair with pale-ish skin. He was always smiling in the pictures with them. The scrapbook was really pretty, and they had different cut outs of shapes. There were photos of them at Disney World and African Safaris. There was a photo of them standing in front of their house, a two-story beige house tucked into the woods. There was a page about their son, Christopher, and what he liked to do. He liked Yugi-Oh cards and Legos. During winter break of my fourth grade year, I thought about it and it did not take me long to come to the decision that I want to be adopted by the Gums.

My visits with Aaron in the laundry room became more frequent when he found out I was getting adopted and held that over my head. I wanted it to stop. A few days later, Miss Jennifer came and I told her that I wanted to meet the Gums. She told me to hold on to the scrapbooks and that I could give them back myself. The day that they were coming, I was so nervous. I made sure that I wore my best clothes, a navy shirt and khakis. Sharon made coffee, tea, and cookies and she told me not to eat until they got there.

The doorbell rang and I was sitting on the couch, holding the scrapbooks on my lap. Miss Jennifer came in first and behind her was Sean and Debbie Gum. They looked just like their photos. Sharon introduced herself and talked about me for a little bit. She said I was a good kid and very smart.

She gave a lot of compliments that I never heard her give before. Shawn and Aaron came from downstairs and said hello. Aaron winked at me before he went upstairs to his room. Debbie asked me how I liked the scrapbooks? I told her that I loved the scrapbooks and I asked her where her son was. She told me he was her stepson and was Sean's son from his first marriage. He only came to visit every other weekend. We talked about school and I told her about the D.A.R.E program that I was in and about being a crossing guard. I told her I was happy to be in a regular class. I asked about schools in her town and where I would go to school. She told me if I decided to make them my "Forever Family" I would go to a private Catholic school and become Catholic. I would have parties and get baptized. We sat and talked for over an hour and at the end they stood up and hugged me. I told them I would like to make them my "Forever Family." I started crying and my tears dropped on the scrapbooks. I wiped off my tears and I tried to hand them to Debbie. She told me to keep them and that I would put them on the family album shelf when I came home.

They left with Miss Jennifer. I went to my room with the scrapbooks thinking of all the vacations we would take, all the places I would visit, and all the things I would see. I thought about becoming Catholic and going to a private school for the first time and wearing a uniform. I thought about having my own room in a big house in the woods with a white picket fence. I dreamed of all these things.

28

The Best Christmas Wish Granted

I didn't have to dream long. Miss Jennifer called and told me that I would get to spend Christmas and New Years with the Gums. The day came and I was bouncing off the walls with excitement. Sharon had been saying negative things to me all week like "Don't get too excited because they probably won't choose you." I did not know why she was upset. Shouldn't she be happy that I was getting adopted? Or was she more concerned about the income she might be losing? Either way, I was not letting anything or anyone take this moment away from me. I sat by the front door with my garbage bag full of clothes looking out of the bay window. Aaron came downstairs from his room and asked me what I was waiting for. I ignored him but Sharon mockingly told him that I was waiting to be disappointed by people who weren't probably going to adopt me.

Aaron came up to me and whispered, "Can't wait for you to get back". He winked and went downstairs to the basement. Tears started swelling in my eyes because I was getting upset and scared they might be right. As soon as the tears came they were gone when I saw the Gum's burgundy Ford Crown Victoria come down the snowy street. "They came!" I kept screaming over and over until Sharon scolded me. I saw Sean and Debbie get out of the car and make their way to the front door and knock. I open the door and gave them both a huge hug. After letting them in, I showed Sean around while Sharon explained to Debbie how to give me my cocktail of medications.

We finally left the Miller's and got on the highway. Debbie was asking me a ton of questions and I was answering them as fast as I could. She told me that she was originally from Chicago and that she met Sean there while teaching inner city kids. She said that is when she knew that she wanted to adopt a child from the inner city. She told me that she was now a Catholic school teacher and Sean owned several successful businesses. I asked her if Christopher, her stepson, would be there when we got to their house. She said that he would be coming in over the weekend. We had been driving for over two hours when Sean pointed out a small sign that said "Welcome to Allegan, Michigan." This is were they lived. It was so different from Detroit or Muskegon. We passed their church, Blessed Sacrament, and Debbie told me we would be going to Mass there on Sunday. We drove down M89 and made two right turns. Sean slowed the car down as he pulled into a partially-shoveled driveway. The driveway was long and winding. At the end of the garage, there was a tan colored, newly built, two-story home with a two-car garage. On the side of the house there was a covered canopy tent with a Go Kart under it.

Sean and Debbie took my hands and walked me up to large wooden front door with crystal windows. The door opened and I immediately noticed the smell of gingerbread cookies and a fire blazing in the large, stone fireplace. Debbie helped me take off my winter coat and boots and put them in the hall closet. "Welcome home," she said as she told me to go explore the house. The house was very colorful with different colors and themes in each room.

The kitchen was yellow and had a sunflower theme. I went downstairs in the basement that was fully finished. There was a large flatscreen TV and couch with video game systems. I ran up two flights of stairs and Debbie was in the master bedroom. I asked her where my bedroom was located and she pointed across the hall. I opened the door and saw a soccer themed bedroom with a lot of Legos and other toys. There was one bed in the middle of the room and a neon green soccer clock that lit up at night. Debbie walked up behind me and let me know that we would redecorate and get another bed because Chris and I would share this room.

That weekend Chris came from his mom's and I got to meet him for the first time. We hit it off right away. Chris was six months older than me but we had the same interests and were in the same grade. Chris was really happy to have someone to play with. He told me it can get lonely way out here in the woods. With me there, we played all day, made snowmen and forts in the woods behind the house. We both also loved video games. I really liked Chris, my new brother.

Christmas morning came and we went to the church we passed. I had never been to a Catholic Church before but it was really weird. They prayed and sang in latin for some parts and there was a lot of kneeling. Debbie whispered explanations of what was happening in ear. She told me once I was adopted I would become Catholic and understand everything.

After Mass, we went home and there was a room full of wrapped presents. I had never seen so many perfectly wrapped presents under one tree before. Sean and Debbie sat on the burgundy leather couch while a fire was blazing and Christmas music was playing. Debbie told me to find my presents and I made my way through the presents. I picked up the first present and it had my name on it. I opened it and it was a Nintendo GameCube! I started jumping up and down with excitement and ran over and gave Sean and Debbie a hug. I asked if I could play it now and Debbie said that I had more presents to open. More! I had never gotten more than two gifts on

Christmas. I opened a smaller gift and it was a Game Boy Advance with the light attachment. Chris also got one and we were ecstatic. We both just kept opening present after present. By the end, the floor was completely swallowed covered with wrapping paper.

Sean got up from the couch and told us to put on our coats. He said there was one more present, the biggest one yet. I was shaking. I didn't know how much more excitement I could take. I put on my coat and ran outside. In the driveway, there a bright blue Go Kart! Sean said that Chris and I could race around the track he built in the woods. I was speechless, a whole Go Kart! That was really mine!

We had a big Christmas dinner and Chris and I played with our new toys. We didn't do much but spend time in the house and outside riding Go Karts. It was the most fun I could remember having. New Years Eve came and it was time for Chris to go back to his moms. I gave him a hug and told him I was glad he was my brother. Debbie let me know that I also would have to go back to the Miller's the next day. I asked her why I couldn't stay and she told me that they had to follow the adoption process. Six monthly visits were required before the final adoption. All of the love and positivity I had been surrounded by the entire week seemed to slip out of my grip and I dreaded going back to the Miller's and have to deal with Aarons abuse. I started screaming and crying and Debbie grabbed me and hugged me tight. She kissed my head and told me not to worry because they would see me soon. In between sobs I told her that wasn't the issue. She asked what the issue was and I shook my head no because I didn't want to tell her. But then, I heard Sharon's and Aaron's voices in my head laughing and teasing me as they did before the Gums picked me up. I started to get angry. I would not let them take this new family from me. I had gotten everything I dreamed of that got me through all of those horrible foster homes. I had to stand for myself and speak up or I might not get another chance. While crying, I looked up and told her that Aaron had been raping me for months and if i didn't do what he wanted I wouldn't get good food. She seemed confused, shocked and upset. She apologized that I went through that and told me she would speak to Miss Jennifer in the morning.

The next morning Miss Jennifer's familiar Pontiac was parked in the driveway when I woke up. Miss Jennifer, Sean and Debbie were all in the dining room talking. I greeted them with a good morning and told Jennifer about my Christmas and all of my presents. She told me that was awesome but asked me to sit. Debbie them asked me to tell Miss Jennifer what Aaron had done. I did and told her I wanted to stay with the Gums. She told me that wasn't possible yet, assured me that I would not be going back to the Miller's. I said, "What about Joe?' Jennifer let me know that she had found a temporary home that will take both Joe and I until my adoption was final and Joe would be placed in a regular foster home.

I guess I didn't have any choice. I did not want to sabotage my chances at adoption by showing misbehavior. Miss Jennifer told me to grab my clothes. I asked Debbie for a trash bag. She went into the basement and came up with a tan suitcase on wheels. She told me I didn't have to live out of a trash bag anymore. I had a home now to pack and unpack at. She helped me put my winter coat on with my boots. And Sean put my suitcase in the trunk. I started crying as we walked to the front door and Debbie wiped my tears. She told me that she would see me next weekend. I said okay and gave her a hug.

While I was hugging her I asked, "Is it okay if I called you mom?"

"Of course," she said. "I am your mom now."

—Karlos Dillard